ASTRONOMY

A LANGUAGE OF ITS OWN

KEY DEFINITIONS IN
ASTRONOMY

JACQUELINE MITTON

FREDERICK MULLER LIMITED
LONDON

First published in Great Britain in 1980 by
Frederick Muller Limited, London NW2 6LE

British Library Cataloguing in Publication Data

Mitton, Jacqueline
    Astronomy. – (Language of its own).
    1. Astronomy – Dictionaries
    I. Title   II. Series
    530'.3   QB14

    ISBN 0-584-10547-9
    ISBN 0-584-10565-7 Pbk

This book is set in 10/11½pt Sabon by
D P Media Limited, Hitchin, Hertfordshire
Printed and bound in Great Britain by
Redwood Burn Limited
Trowbridge & Esher

Preface

Scientists are frequently accused of speaking a language all their own, as if there were a conspiracy to exclude anyone outside their circle. The language of science, though, as with any area of learning or interest, is simply the result of a need to communicate ideas concisely. Astronomy is no exception. Astronomers use words like azimuth and zenith, which are a heritage from Arab skywatchers of a bygone age, alongside terms coined in the 20th century for the exotic objects discovered with ever more sophisticated instruments: quasar, blazar and pulsar, for example.

From among the specialised words astronomers use, I have chosen about 230 terms and names which are the ones most likely to be encountered in a magazine article or television programme, for instance. Celestial objects, famous astronomers and space programmes are included alongside basic terminology. This concise book is not a dictionary, nor an encyclopaedia, so it does not claim to be exhaustive or complete in any sense. It is just a collection of my choice of key words, each of which is explained in non-technical terms. I hope it will help you understand what astronomers are talking about.

Words in **bold type** are used to direct attention to other entries where there will be found further relevant information, or the definition of a technical term.

I am glad to acknowledge the significant contribution made to this book by my husband, Simon, particularly in those subjects where his specialised knowledge fills the gaps in mine.

Cambridge, England   Jacqueline Mitton
1980

A

Aberration (of optical systems)

A deficiency in the performance of an optical instrument, such as a telescope, which causes the image to be less than perfect.

Two types of aberration commonly occur in instruments containing simple lenses: spherical aberration and chromatic aberration. Spherical aberration arises because light falling around the outer part of an ordinary lens is not focused at the same place as light passing through the central portion and hence the image is distorted. It can be corrected by using glass surfaces which are specially figured, and are not simply part of a sphere. The coloured edges often seen around objects viewed through a lens are the result of chromatic aberration. A simple lens acts partly as a prism, splitting the light passing through it into its constituent colours. This problem may be overcome by the use of compound lenses, called achromats. The design of the optical system of a telescope involves compromises because the effects of aberrations can never be completely eliminated, although they must be minimised.

Aberration (of starlight)

A small shift in the apparent position of a star, due to the motion of the Earth in its orbit around the Sun.

The origin of aberration can be likened to the way that rain, actually falling vertically, appears to be driving towards a person moving through it. Similarly, the direction from which a star's light seems to come is affected by the Earth's orbital motion. Aberration was first recognised by James Bradley in 1728. The maximum value of the effect is only just over 20 seconds of arc, for stars viewed in a direction at right angles to the Earth's motion. Light from a star viewed along the direction in which the Earth is moving does not suffer from aberration. As the Earth completes one orbit around the Sun in a year, the net effect of aberration makes the stars appear to move in tiny ellipses around their average positions once a year.

Absolute magnitude see magnitude

Accretion

A process in which a celestial object, such as a planet, is formed or enlarged from a conglomeration of much smaller particles, such as dust.

The accretion idea has received much attention from planetary scientists, as a means by which **planets** may be formed. It is assumed in this theory that the early **Solar System** included a swarm of small fragments (dust, stones, crystals, gas) and that the planets formed from this by accretion. The mutual gravitational attractions of the particles and collisions between them are responsible for smaller particles sticking together and forming larger ones. The eventual result is a handful of large bodies, the planets and their **satellites**. The rocky planets such as Mercury and Mars show a profusion of surface **craters**; these are the record of an intense bombardment by meteorites in the final stages of planetary accretion.

In the 1970s space scientists discovered **binary stars** that are strong X-ray sources and in which accretion can be observed. In these systems gravitational forces cause the outer atmosphere of a **giant star** to be transferred to a dense companion star, such as a **white dwarf**, a **neutron star**, or a **black hole**. The material swirling in towards the dense companion is swung around to form an accretion disc of matter round the dense star. As more matter crashes into the accretion disc it causes intense local heating which makes the disc a strong source of X-rays.

Achondrite see chondrite

Airglow

A very faint light emitted by the upper layers of the atmosphere and caused by radiation from the Sun. It is one of the principal sources of natural background light in the night sky.

Albedo

The reflecting power of objects such as the Moon, and planets.

The albedo is the fraction of light energy falling onto a surface, which is reflected. In the case of a dull object, like the Moon, the figure is around 0.07 or only 7 per cent. In contrast the planet Venus, covered with silvery cloud, has an albedo of 0.75 or 75 per cent.

Algol

One of the most well-known of all variable stars.

Algol is the second brightest star in the constellation Perseus. Its regular changes in brightness arise because it is actually a triple star system in which one star periodically blots out the light from another. It is perhaps the most famous example of an eclipsing **variable star**. Algol is usually **magnitude** 2.2. Dips in brightness down to magnitude 3.5 occur regularly every 2.9 days. The eclipsing pair orbit around the third star in the system, with a period of 1.87 years.

Altazimuth

A type of telescope mounting allowing the tube to be moved independently in **altitude** (swinging on a horizontal axis) and in **azimuth** (swinging round a vertical axis).

Altazimuth mounts are generally used only for small, portable telescopes because they are easy to make. As the stars appear to move slowly through the sky, continuous adjustments in both altitude and azimuth are necessary to keep the telescope pointing at the same object. So altazimuth mounts have generally been impracticable for larger telescopes, especially if they have to be motor driven. Large professional telescopes can, however, be computer controlled and the giant optical telescopes of the future will probably use this mounting. It is already used for some large radio telescopes and for the 6-metre optical telescope of the Soviet Union.

Altitude

The vertical angle between the horizon and an object in the sky, measured along a vertical circle through the object.

See Fig. 3, page 18.

Andromeda nebula

A large, spiral **galaxy**, visible to the naked eye as a misty patch in the constellation Andromeda.

At a distance of about 2,200,000 light years, the Andromeda nebula is the nearest large galaxy to our own. It is a member of what is known as the **"Local Group"** of galaxies. It is the only galaxy visible to the naked eye, but its beautiful spiral structure only becomes evident on photographs taken with the help of large telescopes. Andromeda is a giant among spiral galaxies for it may be twice as massive as the **Milky Way**, and it has a diameter of 125,000 light years or so. It has two dwarf companion galaxies orbiting round it.

Aphelion

The point in the orbital path of a planet or comet where it is furthest from the Sun.

Apogee

The point in the orbital path round the Earth of the Moon or an artificial satellite where it is furthest from the Earth.

Apollo program

Part of the United States' program of space research and exploration. Its objective, to land a man on the Moon and bring him back to Earth safely, was achieved on 20 July 1969 when Neil Armstrong became the first man to set foot on the Moon.

The spacecraft used in the Apollo missions each consisted of three parts: the command module (CM) in which the three astronauts travelled to and from the Moon; the service module (SM) which contained the fuel and engines; and the lunar module in which two astronauts descended to the surface of the Moon while the third remained in the CM, orbiting around the Moon.

Fig. 1. The giant spiral galaxy in Andromeda is accompanied by two small elliptical galaxies. (*Photograph from the Hale Observatories*)

Before the successful landing of Apollo 11, there were several missions to test the system. Then, between 1969 and 1972 there were five further successful trips to the Moon. Many scientific experiments were carried out, including some to detect the **solar wind** and **cosmic rays**. Samples of the Moon rocks and soil were collected for return to Earth. Apollo 13 had to be abandoned following an explosion, though the astronauts all reached Earth safely after a narrow escape. The main details of the Apollo missions are summarised in the Table:

Apollo	Astronauts	Date	Notes
7	Shirra, Eisele, Cunningham	Oct. 1968	test in Earth orbit
8	Borman, Lovell, Anders	Dec. 1968	test in lunar orbit
9	McDavitt, Scott, Schweickart	Mar. 1969	test in Earth orbit
10	Stafford, Young, Cernan	May 1969	test in lunar orbit
11	Armstrong, Aldrin, Collins	July 1969	landing in Mare Tranquillitatis
12	Conrad, Bean, Gordon	Nov. 1969	landing on Oceanus Procellarum
13	Lovell, Swigert, Heise	April 1970	aborted
14	Shepard, Mitchell, Roosa	Jan. 1971	landing at Fra Mauro
15	Scott, Irwin, Worden	July 1971	landing at Hadley Rille
16	Young, Duke, Mattingley	April 1972	landing at Cayley-Descartes area
17	Cernan, Schmitt, Evans	Dec. 1972	landing at Taurus-Littrow area

Apparent magnitude see magnitude

Armillary sphere

A type of celestial globe in which the sphere of the sky is represented by a skeleton framework of intersecting circles, with the Earth at the centre.

Armillary spheres date from the Greek astronomers. They are an attempt to show the way the heavens can be thought of as a sphere surrounding the Earth. The rings used in the framework represent important circles in the sky, such as the **equator** and the **ecliptic.** Some of the rings are movable so that circumstances at different times and different latitudes can be reproduced. On some armillary spheres, the positions of bright stars are shown by small pointers from the fixed rings. Armillary spheres were important devices in antiquity for measuring the positions of the brighter stars.

See also: celestial sphere.

Ashen light

A faint glow sometimes seen on the part of Venus' disc which is not directly illuminated by sunlight when the planet is at a crescent phase.

The origin of the ashen light is uncertain, but it may be produced by a mechanism similar to the **airglow**: the atmosphere itself emitting light when stimulated by atomic particles from the Sun.

Association see star cluster

Asteroids

Small rocky objects which are members of the **Solar System**.

The asteroids are more correctly called minor planets, which describes accurately what they are. They range in size from 1,000 km for Ceres down to a kilometre or so. Many thousands are now recorded by astronomers. Most of them have orbits which lie in the great void between Mars and Jupiter. A few, however, have orbits which carry them much closer to the Earth and the Sun. In 1975 Eros, for example, approached as close as 23 million kilometres (14 million miles). In 1937 the minor planet Hermes came within 780,000 km of Earth. Most asteroids are, fortunately, in orbits which keep them a hundred million kilometres away.

At one time it was thought that the asteroids might be the remains of a shattered planet. However there is nothing like enough material to make even a small planet even allowing for those still undiscovered. It seems more likely that the asteroids are debris left over from the formation of the Solar System. They are basically stony in composition although a few have a more metallic structure. The largest, Ceres, may account for one-third of the total mass of asteroids. Along with **comets** the asteroids are an important reservoir of debris from the early solar system. Collisions between asteroids may be a major source of **meteorites**.

Astrolabe

An ancient instrument for showing the positions of the Sun and bright stars at any time and date.

The invention of the astrolabe is credited to the Greek astronomers who worked about 200 B.C. It consists basically of a circular star map (the "tablet" or "tympan") with a graticule (the "rete") over the top, the two being joined at their common centre, so that the rete can rotate over the tablet. Various engraved scales enable the positions of the stars and Sun to be displayed for any time and date. There may be other scales giving further information. Astrolabes were often fitted with sights so that they could be used to estimate the **altitudes** of the stars, as might be required for navigational purposes. However, the use of any particular astrolabe is restricted to a limited range of latitude for which it is constructed.

Astronomer Royal

Formerly the title of the director of the Royal Greenwich Observatory, but since 1972, an honour bestowed on a distinguished astronomer who is not necessarily the director of the Royal Observatory. The present holder of the title is Sir Martin Ryle.

Astronomers Royal	
John Flamsteed	1675–1719
Edmond Halley	1720–42
James Bradley	1742–62
Nathaniel Bliss	1762–64
Nevil Maskelyne	1765–1811
John Pond	1811–35
Sir George Biddell Airy	1835–81
Sir William Christie	1881–1910
Sir Frank Watson Dyson	1910–33
Sir Harold Spencer Jones	1933–55
Sir Richard Woolley	1955–71
Sir Martin Ryle	1972–

Astronomical unit (abbreviated to A.U.)

The mean distance of the Earth from the Sun. Its value is 1.496 $\times 10^8$ km or about 93 million miles. The astronomical unit is used as a unit of measurement for distances within the **Solar System**. There are 63,240 astronomical units in a light year. A typical subsonic passenger airliner would take around 20 years to travel one astronomical unit.

Atmosphere

The outermost gaseous layers of a **planet, satellite** or **star**.

Not all planets have atmospheres. Only those whose masses are great enough for their gravitational pulls to overcome the natural tendency of gas to expand into space will retain any atmosphere. The planet Mercury, and our Moon, for example, are too small to have any atmosphere. **Venus, Earth** and **Mars** all have atmospheres overlying the solid balls of these planets. The giant planets, **Jupiter, Saturn, Uranus** and **Neptune,** are different from the terrestrial planets in structure, their gaseous layers forming much more substantial parts of their mass. In these cases, the term atmosphere is usually taken to mean the outermost layers, as there is no clearcut boundary in the form of a rocky surface.

Stars, too, are said to have atmospheres, although they consist entirely of hot gas. The stellar atmosphere is used as a term for the thin outermost layer where the features in a star's **spectrum** originate.

Aurora

Luminous curtains or streamers of light seen in the night sky at high northerly or southerly latitudes. They are known as the "northern lights" (aurora borealis) or "southern lights" (aurora australis) according to the place from where they are viewed.

Aurorae occur when electrically charged atomic particles streaming from the Sun get guided towards the polar regions by the Earth's magnetic field, and then collide with the upper layers of the Earth's atmosphere. The magnetic field funnels the particles towards the Earth around latitudes 70°N and 70°S. The energetic particles cause the oxygen and nitrogen in the upper atmosphere to glow. Aurorae are rarely seen in latitudes more than 40° from the poles, except when there is very unusual activity on the Sun.

Solar outbursts, such as intense **flares** near to **sunspots,** eject clouds of high-energy particles into space. Those that reach Earth causes aurorae. It follows that aurorae increase in frequency and intensity as the Sun comes up to its maximum level of activity every eleven years or so.

Azimuth

One of the angular measurements by means of which a position in the sky may be specified. Azimuth is measured around the horizon from North, through East, South and West, to the point on the horizon where a vertical circle through the object intersects it. An object lying due West, for example, has an azimuth of 270°. It is usually used in conjunction with a measurement of **altitude**.

See Fig. 3, page 18.

B

Baily's beads

A phenomenon observed during the progress towards a total eclipse of the Sun, just before totality and again just after totality. As the Moon gradually obscures the disc of the Sun, the final thin crescent appears to be broken up into a string of bright beads, because the mountains of the Moon make its edge uneven, rather than smooth. The English astronomer Francis Baily (1774–1844) drew attention to the phenomenon at the solar eclipse of 1836.

Barnard's Star

The star with the largest known **proper motion**, a value of 10.3 seconds of arc per year.

This ninth magnitude, red star was named after E. E. Barnard (1857–1923) who, in 1916, discovered its comparatively large motion among the stars. It is one of the closest stars to the Sun, being only six **light years** from us. Small, regular fluctuations in its motion have resulted in speculation that it may be accompanied by a planetary system in which a giant planet similar to our Jupiter tugs it off course.

Barred spiral see galaxy

Big Bang

Hypothetical model for the origin of the universe which postulates that all the matter and energy in our universe was concentrated into an unimaginably dense state, or "primeval atom", which has been expanding since the initial "creation event" some 13–20 billion years ago.

The Big Bang is one example of a model from **cosmology**. It is one of the many theories of the universe that have been propounded down through the centuries. At present it is the model that most astronomers would support, inasmuch as present observations suggest that it is more likely to be correct than other models.

The Big Bang theory received a major impetus from the discovery, dating from the 1920s, that the remote **galaxies** are receding from each other, and from the **Milky Way**, at high speeds. This led to the concept of the **expanding universe**. If we back-track the motions of the distant galaxies observed today we inevitably conclude that at some epoch, about 13–20 billion years ago, they were all packed into a single point in **spacetime**. What happened before this we cannot say.

At time zero the universe began to expand, essentially from nothingness, and this expansion has continued ever since. The early stages of the Big Bang are intriguing to physicists and laymen alike. For the first ten-thousandth of a second the universe consisted mainly of sub-atomic particles. By the time the universe was one second old most of the mass we see today had emerged, and many of the sub-atomic particles had been annihilated to produce radiation. This radiation is responsible for the **microwave background radiation**, the discovery of which was a triumph for the Big Bang theory.

Big Dipper see Plough

Binary star

A pair of stars in orbit about each other and held together by their mutual gravitational attractions.

Although our Sun is a solitary star, binary stars and multiple systems of three or more stars are common. About half the "stars" are in fact double or multiple systems, rather than being single. This is not obvious to the casual observer, because most pairs are so close that they cannot be separated by the eye alone. Many binaries are so close that even the world's largest telescopes cannot resolve the two components. Their binary nature has been discovered only through spectroscopy.

The two members of a binary system may be quite different in mass and luminosity, or they may be similar. Their motion is governed by the law of **gravity** and each moves in an elliptical orbit around their common centre of gravity, the balancing point between them. The further apart they are, the slower they move. Binary pairs in which the separation is great enough for them to be seen as separate stars in a telescope often have orbital periods as long as 50 or 100 years. These are called visual binaries. If one of the stars is much fainter than the other, its presence may be revealed only by the obvious orbital motion of its brigher companion. This is an important means of discovery for very faint companion stars such as **white dwarfs**.

As the members of a binary system move in orbit, their velocities towards or away from the Earth change in a regular, repeating pattern. The **Doppler effect** causes regular changes in the apparent wavelengths of features in the spectra of the two stars, revealing their motion. The spectrum of a very close pair contains the light of both stars and careful study of the spectrum may show the binary nature in the first place, and then enable astronomers to deduce what they are like, as well as details of their orbits. Pairs like this are called spectroscopic binaries. They tend to have periods ranging from a day to a few weeks.

Some binaries are so close that the pull of gravity distorts the individual stars from their normal spherical shape. The two stars may exchange material and be surrounded by a common envelope of gas. **Novae** are one of the results of mass exchange in binary stars. At least some X-ray emitting stars are binaries in which mass exchange is taking place and one star is very dense indeed, a tiny invisible **neutron star** or perhaps a **black hole**. The X-ray emission occurs when matter streams onto the dense star.

If the orbits of a binary pair are oriented in space so that one star has to pass in front of the other as seen from Earth, the system is said to be eclipsing. An eclipsing binary star is also a **variable star**. When the light from one of the stars is blotted out by the other one in front of it, there is a drop in the total brightness. The best-known eclipsing system is **Algol** in the constellation Perseus.

Binary stars are important to astronomy because they provide the only generally applicable method for finding the masses of stars. The theory of gravitation, combined with the observations of orbital motion, can give the masses of the individual stars or, if the data is limited, their ratio.

Some pairs of stars which appear to be close together in the sky are not physically connected in any way. They just happen to lie in nearly the same line of sight. Such chance alignments are called optical doubles.

The double star which is most easily observed with the naked eye is the pair formed by Mizar, and its fainter companion, Alcor, in the handle of the **Plough**. When the sky is clear and dark, Alcor is easily visible. However, this is no simple binary system. Mizar has a closer neighbour, visible with a small telescope, and the spectroscope reveals that all three stars are, in fact, spectroscopic binaries. So the Mizar system contains no less than six stars, held together as a family by their mutual gravitational forces.

Black hole

A region of **spacetime** from which light cannot possibly escape.

In his general theory of **relativity** of 1915 Einstein succeeded in demonstrating that the concepts of space, time, mass and **gravity** are inextricably linked. The concept of spacetime, consisting of three spatial dimensions ("length", "breadth", "height") and one time dimension as the basic geometric fabric of the universe, is an essential part of the theory. Matter embedded in this spacetime curves lines that would otherwise be straight, such as the path of a ray of light. This curvature of spacetime is measured by us as a gravitational force.

Once the concept of curved spacetime is accepted one can pose the question: are there regions of spacetime where the curvature is so great that rays of light simply cannot escape? These regions of spacetime, where the severe curvature in the geometry of spacetime prevents light from reaching the exterior, are termed black holes.

In the 1960s theoretical astronomers, stimulated by the discovery of **quasars, pulsars, neutron stars** and X-ray **binary stars**, made major advances in studying the late stages of **stellar evolution**. In particular it was found that stars considerably more massive than the Sun can collapse catastrophically to a state in which they are so tiny that light cannot overcome their intense gravitational fields. If our understanding of the physics of dense matter is correct, then it seems that if the central relic of an old star is more than three solar masses, the formation of a black hole is inevitable. These black holes made by dying stars are only a few kilometres in diameter. One can be detected if it is one member of a close binary system. That indeed seems to be the case for Cygnus X-1, a binary system in which one star is invisible and of about ten solar masses: its presence is revealed by the X-radiation from its **accretion** disc.

Blazar

Very luminous extragalactic object, perhaps a type of **quasar**.
In 1929 astronomers found a variable star in the constellation Lacerta and named it BL Lacertae. Little interest was shown in it until 1972 when it was found to be very similar to the quasars: a distant, highly-luminous, starlike object, showing variability and radio emission. What set BL Lac apart from quasars was the lack of any spectral lines in its **spectrum**. Later, other objects similar to BL Lac were found and they are known collectively as blazars, or lacertids, or as BL Lac objects. Subsequent investigation has suggested that blazars are exceedingly bright and compact cores embedded in elliptical **galaxies**. They are probably generating their energy in a manner similar to the quasars and **radio galaxies**.

Bode's Law

A numerical relationship between the distances of the planets from the Sun, discovered in 1766 by Johann Titius, but more often linked with the name of Johann Bode who published it in 1772. It is not actually a law according to the strict meaning of the word in science, and it may be nothing more than a coincidence.

	Bode's law prediction	Actual distance
Mercury	4	3.9
Venus	7	7.2
Earth	10	10.0
Mars	16	15.2
(Asteroids)	28	(28–33)
Jupiter	52	52
Saturn	100	95.4
Uranus	196	191.8
Neptune	–	300.6
Pluto	388	394.4

The basis of the relationship is the sequence of numbers 0,3,6,12,24,48,96,192,384, in which, after 3, each number is formed by doubling the previous number. If 4 is then added to each member in the sequence, the resulting numbers correspond quite closely with the distances of the planets from the Sun, on a scale in which the Earth's distance is 10 units. The exception to this rule is Neptune, for which there is no Bode number. The value 28 corresponds to no major planet, but the largest asteroid, Ceres, has a distance 27.7 on this scale, and most other asteroids have orbits in this vicinity.

Bolide see fireball

Bolometric magnitude see magnitude

Butterfly diagram

A graphical presentation of the occurrence of **sunspots** on the surface of the Sun through the 11-year solar cycle which results in patches whose shape resembles a pair of butterfly wings.

During the course of a cycle of **solar activity**, the average number of sunspots that can be seen on the Sun at any one time increases to a maximum, then diminishes again. Each individual spot has a fixed position on the Sun, and lasts for a period of weeks. However spots tend to occur preferentially at different solar latitudes, as the 11-year cycle progresses. At the start of a cycle, when there are few spots, they appear in the vicinity of solar latitudes +40° and −40°. As the cycle passes through maximum, and the sunspot numbers then fall again, the zone containing most spots moves nearer to the equator until spots of the new cycle once again erupt at high latitudes.

A graph on which the latitudes of all sunspots are plotted against the date reflects this phenomenon by taking the shape of a pair of butterfly wings. This graph is also known as the Maunder diagram, after the scientist who first plotted it in this form.

C

Carbonaceous chondrite see chondrite

Cassegrain

One of the most common optical arrangements used in reflecting **telescopes**.

The essential feature of the Cassegrain system is a small central hole in the primary mirror. A small, convex secondary mirror near the top of the tube reflects the light from the primary back towards the hole. The light is brought to a focus just behind the primary mirror. This system has the advantage over other possible arrangements that the focus point is easily accessible, being behind the main mirror, and a bulky piece of equipment, such as a **spectrograph**, can be attached there without undue difficulty. The small hole in the primary mirror has a negligible effect on its light-gathering power.

See Fig. 26, page 149.

Celestial sphere

(1) the concept of a large, imaginary sphere, surrounding the Earth, which may be used as a frame of reference for the positions of astronomical objects in the sky; or (2) a globe on which the positions of celestial objects are marked.

Although the stars, planets and other astronomical objects are at different distances from the Earth, this fact is not immediately apparent to the observer, as there is nothing to give any sense of perspective over such vast reaches. For the purposes of referring to apparent positions on the sky and for making maps of the sky, the distances to the stars are irrelevant: all objects may be treated as if they were at the same distance, on the inner surface of a giant sphere around the Earth. Astronomers use a reference grid, comparable with latitude and longitude on the surface of the

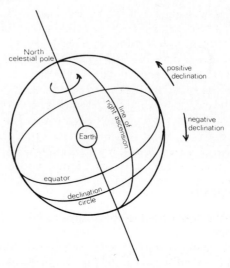

Fig. 2. For the purpose of describing the positions of objects in the sky, an imaginary celestial sphere surrounding the Earth is used. The North and South celestial Poles lie directly above the poles of the Earth and the celestial equator is the projection of the Earth's equator on the celestial sphere. The coordinates most commonly used to specify positions on the celestial sphere, right ascension and declination, are equivalent to longitude and latitude on Earth.

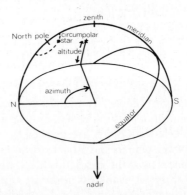

Fig. 3. An observer on the surface of the Earth can see only one half of the celestial sphere at any one time. This half is called the observer's hemisphere. Exactly which half depends both on the observer's latitude, and on the time and date. The height of the pole is simply equal to the observer's latitude. The daily rotation of the Earth causes the apparent motion and the rising and setting of the stars.

Earth, in which the coordinates are **declination** and **right ascension**. The North and South Poles of the celestial sphere lie over the North and South Poles of the Earth, and its equator lies over the terrestrial equator. This system is convenient because the daily rotation of the Earth on its axis makes the celestial sphere appear to turn on an axis through the poles of the Earth. Separations between objects on the celestial sphere are all measured in terms of angles, usually in degrees, minutes and seconds of arc.

An observer on the Earth's surface can see only half of the celestial sphere at any one time, because the Earth itself is in the way. Exactly which half is visible is determined by the observer's latitude, and the time and date.

Cepheid variable see variable star

Charles' Wain see Plough

Chondrite

A type of stony **meteorite**, containing small, spherical mineral bodies, known as chondrules.

Chondrules are typically around 1 millimetre across, and most stony meteorites have them. Those which do not are called achondrites. Among the chondrites is a small class called carbonaceous chondrites, which are remarkable because of the quantities of organic materials they contain. Their overall composition bears a close resemblance to that of the Sun. It is thought that chondrites probably represent the original material from which the Sun and solar system condensed. They probably come to the Earth from the **asteroid** belt. They have been preserved from chemical changes because they have never been heated to very high temperatures.

Chromosphere

Part of the outer gaseous layers of the Sun, visible as a thin crescent of pinkish light in the few seconds immediately before and after the totality of a solar **eclipse**.

The term "chromosphere" arises from the coloured appearance of the layer, in contrast with normal yellow sunlight. It is only during the course of a total eclipse that the overwhelmingly dominant light from the visible disc (**photosphere**) of the Sun is briefly eliminated, allowing the delicate light from this thin layer to be perceived. A **spectrum** of this fine crescent of light, called the flash spectrum, consists of many bright emission lines. One of the strongest is the line produced by hydrogen in the red part of the spectrum, and this is the origin of the chromosphere's colour.

Within the chromosphere the temperature varies from a low value of around 4,500 °K, close to the yellow photosphere of the Sun, up to nearly a million degrees where it merges with the **corona**.

Circumpolar star

A star which never sets, but is always above the horizon from the point of view of an observer at a particular latitude.

Observers in the northern hemisphere can always see some of the constellations close to the North Pole of the sky. The Little Bear, and the Great Bear, for example, are always above the horizon in Europe and North America. Similarly constellations close to the South celestial Pole, such as the Southern Cross, are always visible from Australasia for instance.

The Earth's daily spin on its axis, together with our planet's orbital motion around the Sun, cause the stars to make complete circular paths around the sky in 23 hours 56 minutes 4 seconds. An observer can see only half of the complete **celestial sphere** at any one time. Which half is determined by his latitude, and by the time and date. The observer's latitude governs the altitude of the Pole, which is simply equal to the observer's latitude. When the sky is viewed from the equator, the North and South celestial Poles are due north and due south on the horizon. All the stars seem to rise vertically over the horizon and sweep out semi-circles, passing overhead, and straight down to the opposite horizon.

If an observer were to stand at the North Pole, he would see the Pole Star, which is practically at the North celestial Pole, directly overhead. The apparent rotation of the sky carries the stars in horizontal circles around him. No stars rise or set, and he never gets a glimpse of any of the stars lying south of the celestial equator in the sky.

Most people live in countries at intermediate latitudes. For them, there are some stars which rise and set, and others around the Pole which can always be seen. If the stars were visible in daylight, then the circumpolar stars would seem to trace out complete circles in the sky, centred on the Pole, during the course of a day. A time exposure photograph of the sky around the North or South Pole reveals circular star trails beautifully.

See Fig. 3, page 18.

Cluster of galaxies

A collection of **galaxies** that are physically associated with each other by their mutual gravitational attractions.

The clustering of galaxies on the sky is obvious on any celestial map showing the distribution of galaxies. Many thousands of clusters have been identified and catalogued; some of them are extremely distant. Galaxy clusters vary enormously in population, containing anything between a few tens and thousands of galaxies in a region typically a few million **light years** across. Galaxy clusters are the largest entities which have been certainly identified in the universe.

Fig. 4. A cluster of galaxies called Abell 1060. (*U.K. Science Research Council photograph*)

Clusters of galaxies may be symmetrical, or quite irregular. They may contain a mixture of different types of galaxies, or show a preponderance of one type. Our own **Galaxy** is a member of the small irregular cluster called the **Local Group**.

The nearer, more well known clusters are often known simply by the names of the constellations in which they lie. The Coma cluster is a regular cluster of over 1,000 galaxies in the constellation Coma Berenices, and over 400 million light years away. The Virgo cluster is a large irregular group. Other well known clusters include those in Perseus and Hercules, and in Centaurus in the southern hemisphere.

Clusters of galaxies are of considerable importance in **cosmology** because their brightest members can often be seen even at great distances. The clusters must have formed early in the history of the universe. They are drifting apart from each other, as part of the general expansion of the universe.

X-ray and radio astronomical observations indicate that clusters contain a large amount of hot gas in the space between the member galaxies. The mass of this gas is one of the factors that help to bind together the cluster through gravitational forces.

Cluster of stars see star cluster

Coalsack

A dark area of the sky within the band of the Milky Way and close to the Southern Cross.

Between the myriads of stars which make up the Milky Way lie clouds of gas and dust. Some of this material is dark and opaque, blotting out the light from stars which lie behind it. The Coalsack is the finest visual example of a dark, obscuring cloud, creating what appears to be a gaping hole in the Milky Way. It is visible only in the southern hemisphere, of course.

See also: interstellar matter.

Coelostat

A flat mirror, mounted and motor driven in such a way that it compensates for the apparent motion of the stars, and then constantly reflects a particular area of sky into a fixed piece of apparatus.

The coelostat is useful when light from an astronomical object has to be directed into an immovable instrument. The commonest use of such devices is in solar telescopes, when the term "heliostat" may be used instead.

Coma *1*

An abbreviated version of the name of the constellation Coma Berenices – Berenice's hair.

Coma *2*

A defect in the imaging ability of an optical system, such as a telescope, which results in a point of light appearing to have a shape similar to a quotation mark (').

Coma *3*

The visible head of a comet (see comet).

Comets

Diffuse bodies of dust and gas, moving in orbits within the **Solar System**, and around the Sun, often noted for the long spectacular tails they form on approaching the Sun.

The origin and exact nature of comets is not completely settled by astronomers, although many theories have been proposed throughout the millennia in which they have excited mankind. Every year, dozens of comets are sighted by astronomers. Most of them are so faint that they can only be seen in larger telescopes. Occasionally (perhaps once a decade on average) a comet will attain a brilliancy so great that it can be seen easily with the naked eye. In times past these unexpected appearances of bright comets frequently caused consternation, and they were regarded as evil or benign portents.

The most obvious feature of a bright comet is its tail, which grows spectacularly as the comet approaches the Sun. The tail always streams away from the Sun, this being the result of interactions between the solar radiations and the cometary material. The diffuse head of the comet is often called the coma. Some comets seem to show a small condensation of matter in the head, termed the nucleus.

Fig. 5. Comet Kohoutek, photographed in 1974. (*Photograph from the Hale Observatories*)

Most comets are seen to be travelling on orbits that are parabolic as they swing through the inner Solar System. Since a parabola never closes back on itself, being an open curve, most comets presumably travel on into unknown regions of space. However, some comets happen by chance to pass near enough to the gravitational influence of a planet, usually Jupiter, for their orbits to be modified into elliptical shapes. These comets thus become trapped within the planetary system and they are known as periodic comets. After capture they are usually seen at successive reappearances near the Sun. On every subsequent trip they lose material, and thus become gradually fainter.

Probably the most famous of all periodic comets is **Halley**'s comet. Records of its appearance every 76 years or so can be traced back for some 2,000 years. One apparition, that of 1066, was recorded for posterity on the Bayeux Tapestry. Comets are usually named after their discoverers, but in the case of Halley, the honour went to him for the work he did in linking together the appearances of this great comet, and showing how the theory of **gravity** could be applied to predict its return.

Conjunction

An alignment of bodies in the Solar System.

The planets orbit the Sun at different rates, although their paths, including the orbit of the Earth, all lie close to the same plane. Their motion in the sky against the background of stars is confined to a fairly narrow band of sky. From time to time, two or more planets may appear very close to each other. They are then said to be in conjunction. Planets may also be in conjunction with the Sun or Moon.

The term "conjunction" is also used to describe the position of a planet when it forms a straight line with the Sun and the Earth. The inferior planets, Venus and Mercury, have inferior conjunctions, when they lie between the Earth and the Sun, and superior conjunctions, when they lie on the far side of the Sun. **Superior planets** are said to be at conjunction when they are on the opposite side of the Sun to the Earth.

See Fig. 9 on page 43 and Fig. 10 on page 44.

Constellation

One of the 88 named areas of the sky, which together encompass the whole **celestial sphere**.

The definition of a constellation has changed somewhat in the last hundred years in order to keep up with the needs of astronomers. Originally, the constellations were simply prominent patterns of bright stars which were identified by names from the culture and mythology of various peoples. The Babylonians, Greeks, Chinese and Egyptians, for example, all had their own constellations. The patterns may bear some resemblance to the shapes of the creatures or objects they are named after, though the names were more likely just a means of identifying stars and areas of the sky.

The Greeks listed 48 constellations. These are all in the northern part of the sky. The southern constellations were named in the 17th and 18th centuries. Some constellation names which were in use in former times have since been abandoned.

From the 19th century, as astronomers turned their attention to fainter and fainter stars, those lying on the hazy borderline between two constellations were sometimes assigned to one and sometimes the other according to the whim of the observer, leading to considerable confusion. Finally, in 1925, the International Astronomical Union rigidly defined the boundaries of 88 constellations, making them run along lines of **right ascension** and **declination**. All ambiguity was then removed.

The traditional names of the constellations, including the 48 Greek ones, are still used. Their areas vary greatly. Astronomers use Latin versions of the constellation names, which are internationally recognised.

LIST OF CONSTELLATIONS

Latin Name	English Name	Abbreviation
Andromeda	Andromeda	And
Antlia	Air Pump	Ant
Apus	Bird of Paradise	Aps
Aquarius	Water Bearer	Aqr
Aquila	Eagle	Aql
Ara	Altar	Ara
Aries	Ram	Ari
Auriga	Charioteer	Aur
Boötes	Bear Driver	Boo
Caelum	Sculptor's Chisel	Cae
Camelopardus	Giraffe	Cam
Cancer	Crab	Cnc
Canes Venatici	Hunting Dogs	CVn
Canis Major	Greater Dog	CMa
Canis Minor	Lesser Dog	CMi
Capricornus	Goat	Cap
Carina	Keel	Car
Cassiopeia	Cassiopeia	Cas
Centaurus	Centaur	Cen
Cepheus	Cepheus	Cep
Cetus	Whale	Cet

Latin Name	*English Name*	*Abbreviation*
Chamaeleon	Chameleon	Cha
Circinus	Compasses	Cir
Columba	Dove	Col
Coma Berenices	Berenice's Hair	Com
Corona Australis	Southern Crown	CrA
Corona Borealis	Northern Crown	CrB
Corvus	Crow	Crv
Crater	Cup	Crt
Crux	Southern Cross	Cru
Cygnus	Swan	Cyg
Delphinus	Dolphin	Del
Dorado	Swordfish	Dor
Draco	Dragon	Dra
Equuleus	Foal	Equ
Eridanus	River	Eri
Fornax	Furnace	For
Gemini	Twins	Gem
Grus	Crane	Gru
Hercules	Hercules	Her
Horologium	Clock	Hor
Hydra	Water Serpent	Hya
Hydrus	Water Snake	Hyi
Indus	American Indian	Ind
Lacerta	Lizard	Lac
Leo	Lion	Leo
Leo Minor	Lion Cub	LMi
Lepus	Hare	Lep
Libra	Scales	Lib
Lupus	Wolf	Lup
Lynx	Lynx	Lyn
Lyra	Lyre	Lyr
Mensa	Table Mountain	Men
Microscopium	Microscope	Mic
Monoceros	Unicorn	Mon
Musca	Fly	Mus
Norma	Carpenter's Square	Nor
Octans	Octant	Oct
Ophiuchus	Serpent Holder	Oph
Orion	Hunter	Ori
Pavo	Peacock	Pav
Pegasus	Winged Horse	Peg

Latin Name	English Name	Abbreviation
Perseus	Perseus	Per
Phoenix	Phoenix	Phe
Pictor	Painter's Easel	Pic
Pisces	Fishes	Psc
Piscis Austrinus	Southern Fish	PsA
Puppis	Stern	Pup
Pyxis	Compass Box	Pyx
Reticulum	Net	Ret
Sagitta	Arrow	Sge
Sagittarius	Archer	Sgr
Scorpius	Scorpion	Sco
Sculptor	Sculptor's Workshop	Scl
Scutum	Shield	Sct
Serpens	Serpent	Ser
Sextans	Sextant	Sex
Taurus	Bull	Tau
Telescopium	Telescope	Tel
Triangulum	Triangle	Tri
Triangulum Australe	Southern Triangle	TrA
Tucana	Toucan	Tuc
Ursa Major	Great Bear	UMa
Ursa Minor	Little Bear	UMi
Vela	Sail	Vel
Virgo	Virgin	Vir
Volans	Flying Fish	Vol
Vulpecula	Fox	Vul

Copernicus

A Polish astronomer who lived from 1473 to 1543.

Copernicus is often called "the father of modern astronomy" because he was responsible for the revival of the heliocentric description of the **Solar System**, which gradually gained acceptance in the years after his death. The idea that the Sun, not the Earth, is the centre of the Solar system, and that the planets are all in orbit around the Sun was propounded in his book *De Revolutionibus Orbium Coelestium*. This work was only published in the last years of Copernicus' life as he seemed to lack total confidence in his ideas. The antagonism of the church authorities to this work erupted in the late sixteenth century as Europe became engulfed in religious conflict. Copernicus aimed to give an accurate description of the future positions of planets. He was never able to account precisely for the planetary positions, though he established the essential ideas which Kepler later developed. He reasoned that the daily movement of the skies resulted from the Earth's own rotation.

Nicolaus Copernicus is the Latinised form of the name Mikolaj Kopernik. He was born in Torun, Silesia, now part of Poland, and spent much of his life as a Canon at the Cathedral of Frombork. In addition to astronomy, he studied medicine, and was an able administrator. He was responsible for some basic economic reforms in his country.

The great work of Copernicus is remembered by astronomers in several ways. Copernicus is the name of a conspicuous rayed crater on the Moon. It is also the familiar name among astronomers for the Orbiting Astronomical Observatory, OAO-3. This satellite was in operation during 1973, when the 500th anniversary of Copernicus' birth was being celebrated, hence the name. A Soviet satellite launched in 1973 was also named after Copernicus.

Corona

The outermost layer of the Sun's atmosphere, visible as a halo of pinkish light during a total **eclipse** of the Sun.

The solar corona merges imperceptibly with interplanetary space. It is the hottest part of the Sun that is directly observable, having a temperature of 500,000–2,000,000 °K. Although it is only noticeable during a total eclipse, it can be routinely observed with a coronagraph. This is an optical instrument for producing an artificial eclipse in a solar telescope. Skylab astronauts observed the corona out to 30 solar radii with such an instrument.

The high temperature of the corona arises because its density is low (it consists mainly of free electrons and protons) and yet prodigious amounts of energy are being pumped into it by the **photosphere, flares,** and regions of **solar activity.** The end result is to heat up the diaphanous corona to a million degrees. At this temperature it is readily visible only in X-radiation.

The **Skylab** mission enabled the corona to be intensively studied in the mid 1970s. One major finding was of holes in the corona. These are regions of low temperature and density embedded in the hot corona. They are considered to be a major source of the **solar wind.**

Fig. 6. The solar corona as seen at the total eclipse of the Sun on 7 March 1970. A special filter was used to compensate for the rapid decline in brightness of the corona with distance from the Sun's disc. (*Photograph from High Altitude Observatory, Boulder, Colorado*)

Coronagraph see corona

Cosmic rays

Highly energetic atomic particles travelling through interstellar space with velocities close to that of light.

Cosmic rays are continuously arriving at the Earth's upper atmosphere, but very few of these reach the ground as they collide with the atoms in the atmosphere. The result of the collisions are cascades of secondary cosmic rays, including electrons, muons, neutrinos and gamma rays. The study of primary cosmic rays has to made from satellites, rockets or balloons. They are found to consist of protons, electrons, and atomic nuclei.

It is thought that cosmic rays probably pervade the whole **Galaxy**. Evidence for this idea comes from the gamma rays detected in interstellar space, which are created when cosmic rays collide with the hydrogen gas there. Cosmic rays must have their origin in circumstances which can give them their tremendously high energies. **Supernova** explosions, **pulsars**, **radio galaxies** and **quasars** are possible sources of cosmic rays in the universe.

Cosmogony

The study of the origin of the various celestial bodies.

Advances in knowledge have made this a term that is seldom used by the new generations of astronomers. It is now more usual for theorists to specialise their research in the origin of particular objects such as star formation, the origin of the planets, of the condensation of galaxies. Each of these is an aspect of cosmogony.

Cosmology

The study of the cosmos on the grandest scales, and especially the propounding of theories concerning its origin, nature, structure, and evolution.

A cosmology is a model of the universe. Different cultural traditions will therefore have different cosmologies which reflect the cultural, religious and scientific knowledge of the community. Among cultures that are untouched by Western society, a cosmology may be a very simple concept: the Earth as the major part of the universe, with the gods Sun and Moon circling round it. Modern scientific usage of the term is generally restricted to mathematical and physical theories of the origin and nature of the universe. One example of a modern theory of cosmology is that of the **Big Bang** universe.

Telescopes can now observe very remote objects. These, being far away, teach us about the universe on the largest scales. Thus cosmology also has an observable aspect, in that information of interest to cosmologists is gained by observing remote objects such as **quasars**, as well as the **microwave background radiation**.

Coudé

An optical arrangement used in large, reflecting **telescopes**, which results in a focus at a fixed position, whatever the motion of the telescope.

"Coudé" simply means "bent", a description of the path the light follows between striking the primary mirror and reaching the focus. Two secondary mirrors are required within the main tube, and one or more further reflexions may also be necessary. A certain proportion of the light is lost at every reflexion, which is the main disadvantage of the system when faint objects are to be observed. However, the coudé system is essential for the operation of large **spectrographs** which cannot be moved.

See Fig. 26 on page 149.

Counterglow see zodiacal light

Crab Nebula

The gaseous relic of a star in Taurus that was seen to explode spectacularly on 4 July 1054.

The Crab Nebula is one of the most famous nebulae observable in the northern sky. It was discovered by an Englishman, John Bevis, early in the 18th century. Later, on 28 August 1758, the Frenchman Messier stumbled across it and mistook it at first for the return of Halley's Comet. He later made the **Messier catalogue** of the non-cometary nebulae, and put the Crab Nebula first (M1). The Crab Nebula received its name from the Third Earl of Rosse who, in 1848, drew its tangle of filaments and remarked on its likeness to a crab; he probably had a hermit crab in mind.

Photographs show a tangled web of filaments threading a luminous nebula, at the centre of which is a **pulsar**. The filaments are made of gas, mainly hydrogen, helium, oxygen, nitrogen and sulphur. The white part of the nebula largely comprises high-speed electrons and a magnetic field. The nebula is expanding fast, at about one-tenth the speed of light. This expansion started nine hundred years ago when a star exploded as a **supernova**, casting its outer layers into space to form the nebula and leaving a dense relic, the pulsar.

The pulsar at the centre of the Crab Nebula has a period of 33 milliseconds. It is observable across a huge range of wavelengths from radio, through visible, to gamma-rays; no other pulsar has been monitored over such a wide waveband. The rapid rotation period of this pulsar, 30 times a second, indicates beyond doubt that it is a rotating **neutron star**. It is slowing down, and as it does so it feeds energy into the surrounding nebula.

The Crab Nebula is about 6,500 light years away. As a supernova remnant it is relatively young. Considerable effort has been expended on understanding this nebula because it is the nearest supernova remnant.

Crater

A circular depression in the surface of a planetary body, which may be surrounded by terraced walls and may contain a central peak.

Craters are prominent surface features on the planets **Mercury** and **Mars**, as well as on the **Moon** and other planetary satellites in the **Solar System**. They range in size from a few centimetres up to several kilometres in diameter. It is thought that the heaviest cratering was created early in the life of the Solar System by the impacts of numerous **meteorites**. Volcanic activity is also known to have produced cratering, but to a lesser extent.

Culmination

The passage of a celestial object across the observer's **meridian**. The term "transit" is also applied to this event.

The apparent motion of the sky is due to the Earth's daily rotation on its axis. At culmination, a star reaches its highest altitude in the sky and is due south or north in **azimuth**. **Circumpolar stars** are always above the horizon. They cross the meridian twice during the course of a day, once at upper culmination, once at lower culmination. Other stars can be seen to cross the meridian only once a day.

D

Day

As an astronomical term, the time taken by the Earth to make one turn on its axis relative to the Sun (solar day), or the stars (sidereal day).

The length of the solar day varies slightly throughout the year. To prevent obvious confusion, civil time is based on the "mean" solar day, each of which is of the same length and is divided into 24 hours. Observational astronomers usually make use of sidereal time which readily indicates the part of the sky that is visible. In terms of solar time, the sidereal day lasts 23h 56m 04s.091; about 4 minutes shorter than a solar day. The difference arises because of the Earth's orbital motion around the Sun. During the course of a day, the Earth has moved on in its orbit. It takes about an extra 4 minutes for the Earth to turn completely as viewed from the Sun, after the stars have completed a circle round our sky.

Declination

A coordinate, used with **right ascension,** to specify the position of an astronomical object on the **celestial sphere.** Declination is the angular distance from the celestial equator, and is equivalent to latitude on the globe of the Earth.

Declination and right ascension are the coordinates used most regularly by astronomers for specifying positions. Circles of constant declination are parallel to the celestial equator, which has declination 0°. Declinations north of the equator are counted positive, and those south as negative. The North celestial Pole thus has declination +90° and the South Pole declination −90°.

See Fig. 2 on page 18.

Deferent see epicycle

Dichotomy

The point of exact half-phase of the Moon (i.e. half Moon) or a planet. As viewed from the Earth, only Venus and Mercury among the planets can be observed at dichotomy since their orbits round the Sun lie inside the Earth's. At this phase, exactly half of the visible disc is illuminated by the Sun, the other half being in shadow.

Doppler effect

The change in the observed frequency of sound or light waves when the source of waves and the observer are moving towards or away from each other.

The most common illustrations of the Doppler effect occurs when a whistling train or an ambulance blasting a siren shoots by. The pitch of the sound drops suddenly in the instant when the vehicle passes the listener. This phenomenon can be understood quite simply. As the source of sound approaches, it compresses the sound waves more closely in front of it so that they appear to be arriving more frequently. The pitch (i.e. frequency) seems raised. When the source is receding it drags out the waves, so they reach the listener less often. The frequency and the pitch drop. Exactly the same effect occurs if it is the listener moving, rather than the source of sound.

Light waves and electromagnetic radiation in general also display the Doppler effect. This is one of the most important phenomena available to astronomers for revealing the motion of astronomical objects. The frequency change in light shows up as a change in the expected colours of features in the **spectrum** of an astronomical object. A star whose motion is bringing it nearer to the Earth will have all the features in its spectrum shifted towards the blue end. The light from a receding star suffers a red shift.

Redshift has become an important concept in astronomy since the discovery of the **expanding universe** and the **Hubble Law**. The Doppler effect reveals the recession of all the distant **galaxies**.

The situations in which astronomers can take advantage of the Doppler effect for advancing their knowledge of the universe are numerous. For example it may be used to detect **binary stars** which otherwise would be unresolvable. It can show up the motion and structure of the spiral arms of our **Galaxy**, via their radio emission.

Double star see binary star

Dwarf

A term often applied to typical stars, such as the Sun, which have not yet advanced in their evolution to the giant stage.

The term "dwarf" is applied to almost all stars which are not classified as **giants** or **supergiants**. Essentially, the dwarf stars form the main sequence in a **Hertzsprung-Russell diagram**. Some stars which are a little less luminous than the main sequence are called subdwarfs. The **white dwarfs** are a completely distinct group, very much fainter than main-sequence stars of similar temperatures.

See also: star.

Dwarf galaxy see galaxy

Dwarf nova see nova

E

Earth

The third major planet from the Sun in the Solar System.

Unlike any of the other planets, Earth is available for extensive and direct observation and experimentation by man, at close quarters. Inevitably, more is known about the Earth than any other planet, but in an astronomical context, the major features of Earth as a planet can be summarised for comparison with other members of the Solar System.

Earth is the only planet with extensive oceans and the only one with life (with the possible exception of micro-organisms on Mars). The influence of our weather has dramatically altered the surface, but there is some evidence of cratering in the distant past, like that suffered by the Moon, Mercury, Venus and Mars. The atmosphere when dry consists of 78 per cent nitrogen, 21 per cent oxygen, 0.9 per cent argon with traces of other gases, but there are of course variable amounts of water vapour.

The interior structure of the Earth has been deduced from studies of earthquake shock waves as they travel through the planet. A thin crust, some 30 km thick, overlies the mantle which extends to a depth of about 3,000 km and is thought to be composed primarily of silicate rocks. The core is thought to be mainly iron and nickel, which would explain the mean density of the Earth, 5,500 kg per m^3. The outer part of the core, at least, is liquid, though the inner core may be solid, and the interior temperature may be as high as 6,400 °K. Volcanic activity and earthquakes are evidence of continuing instability in the Earth's structure.

Electric currents flowing in the metallic core may be responsible for the Earth's magnetic field. The Earth's field is similar in nature to that produced by a bar magnet, with a pole at either end. At present the axis through the magnetic poles is inclined at 12° to the rotation axis, but in the past the Earth's field has changed many times, including complete reversals.

Earth has one natural satellite, the Moon. Our Moon is unusually large since, among the terrestrial planets, Mercury and Venus have none, and Mars has only two tiny captured asteroids. By contrast, the Moon (diameter 3,476 km) is nearly a quarter the Earth's size. It seems likely that the Earth and Moon are essentially a double planet, both having been formed independently.

See also: Solar System for table of planetary data.

Earthshine

A faint illumination of the dark part of the Moon's disc when it is new, or at the crescent phase.

The origin of this light is sunlight reflected from the Earth to the Moon. The popular term for the phenomenon is "The old Moon in the new Moon's arms".

Since the era of space travel, the term earthshine has another application. The Earth itself is made visible by the sunlight it reflects – presumably earthshine.

Eclipse

The total or partial disappearance from view of an astronomical body when it passes directly behind another object; or the passage of a planetary body through the shadow cast by another object so that it is unable to shine as it normally does by reflected sunlight.

The Moon's orbit around the Earth is inclined at only 5° to the plane of the Earth's orbit around the Sun. From time to time, the three bodies become aligned, and an eclipse of the Sun or Moon occurs.

An eclipse of the Sun can only occur at new Moon, when the Moon lies directly between the Earth and the Sun. Though the Moon is much closer than the Sun, a coincidence of nature makes the apparent sizes of the Sun and Moon nearly equal, at about ½°. It is thus just possible for the Moon to obliterate the Sun briefly. A total eclipse of the Sun lasts 7½ minutes at most at any one place on the Earth; usually the duration is only half this. The Moon's shadow is only a few kilometres wide, and it traces out a curved path across the surface of the Earth as the motion of the three bodies makes the eclipse become visible at successive places. A partial eclipse will be visible in wider regions either side

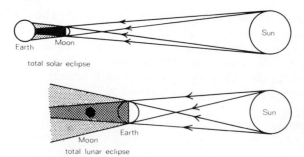

Fig. 7. The relative positions of the Sun, Earth and Moon when lunar and solar eclipses occur. (Diagram not to scale)

of the path of totality. Partial eclipses may occur when no part of the Earth witnesses a total eclipse. Sometimes the Moon is further away from the Earth than average at an eclipse, so its apparent diameter is less than the Sun's. The Moon's dark disc crosses the Sun leaving a bright ring all round. In these circumstances the eclipse is described as annular (like a ring). During the brief moments of a total eclipse of the Sun, the Earth grows dark and animals behave as if it were nightfall. The faint outer parts of the Sun, the **chromosphere** and the **corona**, become visible.

FORTHCOMING TOTAL SOLAR ECLIPSES

Date	Area of visibility of totality
1981 July 31	Black Sea
1983 June 11	Indian Ocean
1984 Nov. 22	New Guinea
1985 Nov. 2	South Pacific
1986 Oct. 3	West of Iceland
1988 Mar. 18	Indian Ocean
1990 July 22	Baltic Sea

An eclipse of the Moon occurs when the Moon passes into the shadow of the Earth. Lunar eclipses can only happen at full Moon as the Moon has to be on the opposite side of the Earth to the Sun. A lunar eclipse can be seen from anywhere on the Earth where the Moon has risen over the horizon. The Moon does not disappear completely, but takes a deep reddish hue from light scattered in the Earth's atmosphere. Eclipses of the Moon are of little interest to lunar scientists but are keenly watched by amateur astronomers.

FORTHCOMING LUNAR ECLIPSES

Date	Extent
1981 July 17	partial
1982 Jan. 9	total
1982 July 6	total
1982 Dec. 30	total
1983 June 25	partial
1985 May 4	total
1985 Oct. 28	total
1986 April 24	total
1986 Oct. 17	total

The moons of other planets in the Solar System may be eclipsed when they pass into the shadow of their primary planet. When such a moon is actually hidden behind the disc of its planet, it is said to be occulted. Similarly, when a star is hidden by the Moon, it is said to undergo an occultation rather than an eclipse. To some extent there is a confusion between the two terms, because a **binary star** system in which one star is periodically hidden behind another is said to be eclipsing, not occulting.

See Fig. 6, page 30.

Eclipsing variable see variable star, binary star

Ecliptic

An imaginary great circle around the sky which is the projection of the Earth's orbit around the Sun onto the **celestial sphere**. This circle is also the Sun's path through the stars as it apparently circuits the sky once a year. The constellations through which the ecliptic passes form the **zodiac**.

The word ecliptic is derived from the fact that eclipses of the Sun or Moon can only occur when the Moon's path crosses the ecliptic. The orbits of the Moon and planets (apart from Pluto) all lie close to one plane, so the Moon and planets are never far from the ecliptic in the sky. The plane of the **Solar System** is sometimes loosely called the ecliptic.

The Earth's rotation axis is inclined at an angle of 66½° to its orbit round the Sun. As a consequence, the ecliptic and the celestial equator are inclined at 23½° on the celestial sphere. These two great circles cross in two places. The point where the

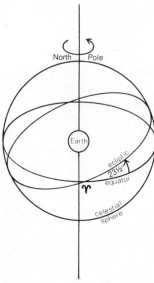

Fig. 8. The ecliptic, the Sun's yearly path around the celestial sphere, is inclined at an angle of 23½° to the celestial equator. The point where the two cross is called the First Point of Aries and is represented by the symbol ♈. This point is taken as the zero for right ascension.

Sun crosses from south to north of the equator is called "the First Point of Aries" and is often signified by the symbol for Aries, ♈. This point is also known as the vernal **equinox**, since the Sun reaches it on approximately March 21 (northern hemisphere spring) and the hours of daylight and darkness are roughly equal. The other point of intersection between the ecliptic and the equator is the autumnal equinox, reached by the Sun on about September 23.

The vernal equinox is taken as the zero point for the scale of **right ascension**, but the equinoxes are not fixed points in the **constellations**. The effects of **precession** cause the equator to slide westwards along the ecliptic, taking around 26,000 years for a complete circuit of the sky. Star maps which include scales of right ascension and declination have to state for which year the scale is correct and usually this is put in the form "correct for the equinox of 1950" (or whatever year is appropriate). As the change is so slow star maps remain usable for many decades.

Electromagnetic radiation see spectrum

Elliptical galaxy see galaxy

Elongation

A term which describes the position of a planet, or the Moon, in its orbit, relative to the Sun as seen from the Earth. It is defined as the angle formed between a line joining the Earth to the planet (or the Moon) and a line from the Earth to the Sun.

Certain elongations are given special names: elongations of 0°, 90° and 180° are called conjunction, quadrature and opposition, respectively. The planets Mercury and Venus, whose orbits lie inside the Earth's, appear to oscillate from one side of the Sun to the other as we view their orbital motion. The greatest elongation Mercury ever achieves is 28° and Venus' elongation never exceeds 48°. The greatest elongation reached by either of these planets, east or west, on any particular oscillation depends on the exact circumstances, and may not be the maximum possible. The Moon and the remaining planets may be viewed at any elongation between 0° and 360°.

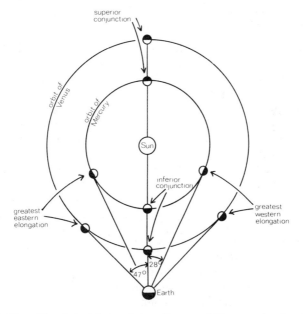

Fig. 9. The orbits of the inferior planets, Venus and Mercury, showing their positions relative to the Earth at conjunctions and greatest elongations.

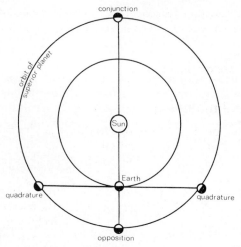

Fig. 10. The orbit of a superior planet showing its position relative to the Earth at conjunction, opposition and quadrature.

Ephemeris

(1) a tabulation of the positions on the **celestial sphere** of the Sun, Moon and planets. Such tables are usually produced annually for the benefit of astronomers and navigators and are also known as almanacs. They often include useful additional information on the relations between different systems of time, phenomena such as eclipses, locations of major observatories, and data on bright stars.

(2) a table of predictions, generally at regular intervals of time, of the expected path on the celestial sphere of a moving object, particularly a comet.

The plural form of ephemeris is ephemerides; the word is derived from a Greek noun meaning a diary.

Epicycle

A small circle, the centre of which moves along a larger circle termed the deferent.

Epicycles are encountered in Earth-centred models of the universe. They are a mathematical device ("wheels within wheels") that enables the complex planetary motions to be reproduced approximately, if it is supposed that a planet is fixed to a rotating epicycle that also moves along a large circle. Epicycles were an essential feature of the **Ptolemaic** model of the Solar System, which was finally overturned by **Copernicus** in 1543.

Equator see celestial sphere

Equatorial mounting

Method of mounting a telescope so that it can be moved independently in either **right ascension** or **declination**.

In this system one axis, the polar axis of the mounting, is parallel to the Earth's rotation axis. Motion of the telescope about this axis alone is sufficient to cancel out the apparent daily rotation of the sky. The problem of keeping the telescope locked onto a particular star is therefore made relatively easy, especially for a small amateur telescope where a simple electric motor with reduction gears can be employed. The second axis, the declination axis, is at right angles to the polar axis. The declination axis is usually clamped once a star has been located, and, with the polar axis drive switched on, the desired object will be held in the field of view. Many professional telescopes, such as the 5-metre Hale telescope and the 4-metre Anglo-Australian telescope, use the equatorial system. Its dominance may be challenged in the next generation of giant telescopes, which are likely to use **altazimuth** mountings instead.

Equinox

(1) One of the two points on the **celestial sphere** where the **eliptic** intersects the celestial equator.

(2) One of the two occasions in the year when the hours of daylight and darkness are of equal duration. To within a day, this happens on March 21 and September 23 each year, when the Sun's path crosses the equator.

Escape velocity

The minimum speed that an object must attain in order to escape the gravitational pull of a massive body, such as a planet or star.

In order to escape from the gravity of a massive body, an object has to move against the gravitational force and this results in a loss of energy. To beat the gravitational field it must have enough energy in its motion to offset this loss, otherwise it will fall back towards the massive body. Once escape velocity is attained, however, no further energy needs to be supplied; if the escaping object is a rocket, its engines can shut down and it will still coast away even though it will slow down as the gravitational force continues to act on it. For the Earth the escape velocity is 11 kilometres per second, which is why massive booster rockets are needed for space travel that commences at its surface. On the Moon, a less massive body, the escape velocity is only 2.5 kilometres per second, whereas for the Sun it is a little over 600 kilometres per second. The largest escape velocities are associated with **black holes**, regions of **spacetime** where the escape velocity exceeds the velocity of light.

Evening Star

Usually the planet Venus when seen in the west after sunset. Mercury is also described as being an "evening star" when it is visible after sunset.

When Venus is near its greatest eastern elongation it is a brilliant object (magnitude -4.4), brighter than any other planet or star, and is seen in a comparatively dark sky. Mercury is much harder to locate, being fainter and closer to the Sun.

Expanding universe

An interpretation of the observed recession velocities of galaxies as an overall expansion of the universe itself.

The idea that the entire universe is in a state of expansion was put forward in 1929 by Edwin Hubble. In the early part of the 20th century astronomers had begun to notice that the **redshifts** of **galaxies** indicated that the great majority of them are moving away from us. In 1917, W. de Sitter, who was applying Einstein's general theory of **relativity** to **cosmology**, developed a model in which material "particles" (galaxies for example) repel each other. This model, which is almost certainly wrong, introduced the notion of an expanding universe. By 1929 Hubble had discovered **Hubble's Law**, which showed that the velocity of recession of a galaxy increased with distance. This steady increase of velocity with distance may be interpreted as the expansion of the universe.

It is the **Big Bang** model of **cosmology** that gives a natural explanation of the expanding universe, in which we view cosmic matter that is still rushing away from the initial expansion in spacetime.

Relativity theory shows that the expansion may be considered as a property of **spacetime** itself. The scale of actual coordinate network of space and time is expanding, or, to say it another way, the scale of the "graph paper" of spacetime is steadily growing. **Clusters of galaxies** are points locked into this expanding framework of spacetime and they, therefore, act as beacons of the expansion. It is important to realise that within a galaxy cluster, within a galaxy, within a star, planet or satellite, the distances between objects or their atoms are *not* increasing. Only on the grandest scale of the universe, that of entire clusters of galaxies, does the expansion affect the distances between the "particles" – in this case galaxy clusters.

Another frequent misconception is that we must be at the centre of the expansion. In fact the expanding universe would look essentially the same on the grand scale from every viewpoint. To see that this is so, imagine a balloon with a pattern of dots on it. As the balloon is blown up the distances between dots increase; every dot sees all other dots at ever-increasing distances, yet no dot is at the centre of expansion. The two-dimensional surface of the balloon is expanding in three-deminsional space. Similarly, the expansion of the three spatial dimensions of the universe has to be treated as a process in the four-dimensions of spacetime, whose centre, at the instant time equals zero, is the onset of the Big Bang.

F

Faculae

Active regions on the Sun that appear bright compared to the surrounding **photosphere**.

The faculae are bright patches in the upper part of the photosphere. They are one manifestation of a region of **solar activity** and occur where the magnetic field has been enhanced, usually by magnetism spewing out of the solar interior. Faculae are often seen in the immediate neighbourhood of **sunspots**.

Field star

An individual star which is not a member of a cluster or **association**.

The term is often used to distinguish between the members of a **star cluster**, or stars belonging to a **galaxy** under study, and the stars which happen to lie in the same line of sight, but are closer, and do not belong to the object being studied.

Fireball

A particularly brilliant **meteor**.

A meteor has to achieve a **magnitude** of about -10 before it qualifies as a fireball. Fireballs are of interest to **meteorite** hunters, since meteorite falls are usually associated with very bright meteor flashes. Observations of the path followed by a fireball as seen from different locations may be used to predict the area in which any fall of meteoritic material probably landed. Occasionally a brilliant fireball may be accompanied by a loud explosive sound, in which case it is known as a bolide.

First point of Aries

One of the points where the **ecliptic** and the celestial equator intersect. It is the zero point for the **right ascension** scale. The Aries symbol, ♈, is used to represent this intersection, even though the effects of **precession** have moved it into the constellation Pisces. The term "vernal **equinox**" is also applied to this point in the sky, as it is the Sun's position at the equinox occurring in spring in the northern hemisphere.

See Fig. 8, page 42.

See also: celestial sphere.

Flare

An energetic outburst in the lower atmosphere of the Sun.

Solar flares are one of the most spectacular aspects of **solar activity**. Flares occur in active regions of the Sun, which can be pictured as zones in the Sun's surface layers where the intense magnetism of the interior is trying to break out. Flares are seen as bright flashes of light in the active region and extending over considerable areas. They may last from seconds to tens of minutes. The flare itself may be imagined as a powerful discharge releasing pent-up electromagnetic energy. Clouds of electrically-charged atomic particles are flung into space. Those that reach the Earth can temporarily disrupt radio communications and they are largely responsible for impressive **auroral** displays.

Fraunhofer lines

Narrow, dark absorption lines cutting across the continuous **spectrum** of the **Sun**. The term is also applied to similar lines found in the spectra of other stars.

Fraunhofer lines are named after Joseph von Fraunhofer, who first studied these features in 1814. With his limited equipment, he identified several hundred lines. Some of the strongest he designated by letters of the alphabet, using both upper and lower case letters. These letters are still commonly used by spectroscopists.

ABSORPTION LINES IN THE SOLAR SPECTRUM, LETTERED BY FRAUNHOFER

Wavelength (nm*)	element responsible	letter	notes
759	oxygen	A	produced in
687	oxygen	B	Earth's own Atmosphere
656	hydrogen	C	Hα
590	sodium	D1	
589	sodium	D2	
527	iron and calcium	E	
518	magnesium	b1	
517	magnesium	b2	
517	magnesium	b4	
486	hydrogen	F	Hβ
434	hydrogen	G	Hγ
397	calcium	H	
393	calcium	K	

*nm = nanometre = 10^{-9} metre

Fraunhofer thought that the dark lines might be created in the Earth's atmosphere. However, since other stars show patterns of lines quite different from the Sun's this is impossible as a complete explanation. Some Fraunhofer lines are created in the Earth's atmosphere, but most originate in the outer layers of the Sun. Gas atoms are capable of absorbing light at sharply defined wavelengths (colours). Different elements absorb different sets of wavelengths, and so imprint their identity on the spectrum. The strengths of the Fraunhofer lines in the solar spectrum are used to determine the chemical composition and physical conditions in the Sun's outer layers.

G

Galactic cluster see star cluster

Galaxies, cluster of see cluster of galaxies

Galaxy, The

The Galaxy is the huge star family to which our Sun belongs and which we see as the **Milky Way**.

The Sun is just one star in the Galaxy; there are about 100 billion stars altogether in this system, which forms a giant spiral **galaxy**. It is conventional to distinguish our Galaxy in particular from galaxies in general by writing it as a proper noun with a capital G. The Milky Way is the background light of the myriads of stars in our home Galaxy.

In shape the Galaxy is basically a flat disc with a bulge, the nucleus, in the centre. Its diameter is about 100,000 **light years**. The nucleus is about 10,000 light years thick, and elsewhere the disc is about 1,000–2,000 light years thick. Within the disc of the Galaxy there are **stars** and **interstellar matter**. Superimposed on a general distribution of stars and gas clouds within the disc is a system of two spiral arms that emerge from the nuclear region. They can be traced right round the Galaxy. Our Sun is located some 33,000 light years from the galactic centre and is within one of the spiral arms. The Galaxy as a whole rotates, but not rigidly like a wheel. The central regions are a swirling mass of stars and gas, taking as little as a million years to circle once. Further out the rotation speed drops. At the Sun's distance from the centre it requires about 250 million years for one orbit to be completed. The speed of the Sun's motion due to galactic rotation is about 250 kilometres per second.

Surrounding the disc there is a spherical halo containing the **globular clusters**. These ancient star families mark out the shape that the Galaxy had when it first formed, in the early universe, some 13–20 billion years ago. As the gas in the Galaxy collapsed under its own gravity to form a swirling disc, the globular clusters were left stranded – a cosmic fossil telling us of the Galaxy's original shape.

There are uncounted billions of spiral galactic systems like ours throughout the universe. An important feature of our Galaxy, however, is its sheer size. It is one of the largest spiral galaxies known, although elliptical galaxies may be considerably more massive.

Infrared astronomy and **radio astronomy** have made important contribution to the study of our Galaxy as a whole. The Sun is buried in the disc and, as a consequence, the optical astronomers' gaze is cut short after a few thousand light years by heavy obscuration caused by interstellar matter. The infrared and radio waves penetrate this haze readily. Infrared studies have revealed unexpected energetic activity at the heart of the Galaxy and it has even been suggested that a central black hole may be responsible. Radio maps reveal a fast-spinning disc of hydrogen at the centre and two expanding arms that may have been cast out in an explosion 10 million years ago.

Fig. 11. A barred spiral galaxy, NGC 1300. (*Photograph from the Hale Observatories*)

Galaxy

A giant family of stars which is held together by its own gravitational force. The **Milky Way** is our own huge **Galaxy**, containing perhaps 10^{11} stars in all. Most of the material universe is organised into galaxies of stars.

Galaxies come in a great variety of forms. The important distinguishing feature is that the stars, gas, and dust within a particular galaxy constitute one system that is almost gravitationally independent. So, the huge globular **star clusters** containing a million stars do not qualify as galaxies in their own right because their behaviour is dominated by the gravitational fields of their parent galaxies. On the other hand, the Milky Way is quite definitely a galaxy, for it is separated by two million light years – twenty times its own diameter – from its nearest comparable neighbour. In fact when written with a capital G, the word Galaxy always denotes our own family of stars, the Milky Way.

The first generation of large telescopes, used by Herschel for example, could not discriminate between the starry nature of distant galaxies and the hazy clouds of interstellar matter within our Galaxy. For this reason the galaxies are occasionally called extragalactic nebulae, a name in common use until about 1950.

It is helpful first to divide the galaxies into three groups in order to discuss their properties: spirals, ellipticals and irregulars. Within these broad classifications further subdivisions may be used.

Spiral galaxies are flat discs of stars with two spiral arms emerging from the central region. They account for about one-quarter of all galaxies, although they are the dominant form among the brighter galaxies. There are normal spirals and barred spirals; in the latter the two arms are apparently attached to a bright central bar of stars. Spirals are well supplied with interstellar material. The rotating spiral pattern compresses this gas and dust and so triggers the formation of bright new stars within the arms. Within the spiral arms, therefore, we find young stars. Examples of spiral galaxies discussed elsewhere are the **Andromeda Nebula** and the Galaxy.

Elliptical galaxies as their name suggests have a symmetrical elliptical or spheroidal shape with no obvious structure. Their stars are all very old, for these galaxies are almost devoid of interstellar material and so they cannot benefit from star birth. The very brightest galaxies of all are giant ellipticals with masses approaching 10^{13} solar masses; and the tiniest galaxies, no bigger than globular clusters, are ellipticals with a million members. The observed shapes vary from spheres to melon-shaped galaxies that are about three times longer than their own width. Approximately two-thirds of all galaxies are ellipticals.

Irregular galaxies are the one-tenth of the population that do not fit the spiral or elliptical pattern. These are discussed below.

Why do galaxies have spiral or elliptical shapes? This question has taxed theorists for a century or more. Although it is now quite certain that spirals do not change into ellipticals, precisely what does happen is unclear. The two major types have formed differently and evolve differently. It is possible that in the early stages of galaxy formation some galaxies managed to retain their interstellar material while others blasted it into intergalactic space during a furious epoch of rapid star formation. The galaxies that hold onto their gas subsequently collapsed to discs (spirals) whereas those that lost their gas retained the elliptical form.

Most galaxies are extremely old. It is hard to give precise estimates. Our Galaxy is at least twelve thousand million years old, and this is typical of most galaxies. (Our Sun is five thousand million years old.)

The distances to galaxies are incomprehensibly large. The nearby **Magellanic Clouds** are 180,000 light years away. A cube with sides a few million light years long contains the members of the **Local Group**. The next significant cluster of galaxies is tens of millions of light years away. The most distant luminous objects seen by telescopes are possibly ten thousand million light years away; at that distance only superbright supergiant 'galaxies' are visible, and then only as smudges and specks on photographs or TV scanners. It is precisely because galaxy clusters are visible at such great distances that they are of major importance in observational **cosmology**, since it is necessary to look deep into the universe in order to determine its geometrical structure.

The final fate of galaxies is something about which one can only speculate. As aeons pass greater proportions of the galactic material get locked up in stellar dead ends: **white dwarfs**, **neutron stars** and **black holes**. Star formation slows down, and ultimately must cease on account of a lack of interstellar matter. If any massive black holes form these will grow by capturing dead stars that stray too close. Ultimately the galaxy might be nothing more than a giant invisible black hole.

In studying the extragalactic universe astronomers have found many interesting types of galaxy and given them a variety of names. Types are named after the discovery technique (e.g.

radio galaxy), discoverers (e.g. Seyfert galaxy), or by catalogue name (e.g. 3C84). Brief notes on some of the more important types follow.

Haro galaxies: objects with unusual spectra catalogued by Haro working in Mexico.

Maffei galaxies: two members of the Local Group found by Paolo Maffei in 1968.

Markarian galaxies: objects with unusual spectra found by B. E. Markarian working at Byurakhan Observatory in Armenia.

Seyfert Galaxies: spiral galaxies with brilliant nuclei and faint arms, named after Carl Seyfert who defined them in 1943. These are also radio galaxies.

Zwicky galaxies: compact galaxies noted in several catalogues by the Swiss-American Fritz Zwicky. They are barely distinguishable from stars on **Schmidt** photographs.

Exploding and interacting galaxies: loosely descriptive terms applied to galaxies that appear to have exploded or be entwined with neighbours. Detailed study of particular systems has sometimes disclosed, however, that the dramatic photographic images are illusions.

N-type galaxies: similar to Seyferts, but almost no trace of spiral arms.

Quasars are discussed separately; they are related to radio galaxies.

Radio galaxies: galaxies that are strong sources of radio waves. About one galaxy in a million is a strong radio source. They are important astrophysically because the energy emerging as radio flux is exceedingly large, as much as 10^{38} watts for the most energetic ones. Radio maps often show two clouds of radio emission symmetrically disposed on either side of an optically visible galaxy. In the most extreme examples the two radio clouds may be separated by a few million light years.

Blazars are discussed separately; they may be related to quasars and radio galaxies.

Astrophysically the active galaxies mentioned above are of considerable importance. In such galaxies the non-stellar energy, in the form of radio waves, light, X-rays, or infrared rays, may greatly exceed the energy given out by the normal stars. In our own Galaxy the stars dominate. Apparently there are rare cases where this is not so, and it is important to discover the underlying causes of this non-stellar energy.

See Fig. 1 on page 5 and Fig. 4 on page 21.

Galileo Galilei

An Italian astronomer who lived from 1564 to 1642.

Galileo was the first astronomer to publicise the results of turning a telescope on the sky, and so was able to announce many new discoveries. The first commercial telescopes were made by Dutch opticians; when news of the invention reached Galileo, he made one for himself (1609). His simple design, consisting of two lenses, is still known as a Galilean telescope. Among the many sights which the telescope revealed to Galileo were the mountains and craters on the Moon and four moons circling the planet Jupiter. These four are known collectively as the Galilean moons, and have the individual names Io, Callisto, Europa and Ganymede.

Galileo made many contributions to mechanics and he is said to have performed a famous experiment at the top of the well known Leaning Tower in his birth-place, Pisa. He is supposed to have dropped simultaneously two weights, a large one and a small one, demonstrating that they reached the ground at the same time.

Galileo's discoveries convinced him of the truth of the Sun-centred model of the **Solar System** put forward by **Copernicus**. Unfortunately for him, the climate of opinion in the church regarded this view very unfavourably, and in his later years he was forced into silence.

Gamma ray astronomy

Beyond the X-ray region of the **spectrum** lies the gamma ray region which can be explored by astronomers using detectors launched above the Earth's atmosphere.

Gamma rays have wavelengths at least a million times shorter than visible light, and they are the most energetic form of electromagnetic radiation. They can only be detected above the Earth's atmosphere because they are absorbed by air. Gamma rays are created only under extreme conditions, such as those encountered in violently explosive phenomena. For example, gamma rays released by nuclear reactions in solar **flares** have been detected. The **pulsar** in the **Crab Nebula** is a strong source of gamma rays, and so are a few energetic **galaxies** and **quasars**.

Gegenschein see zodiacal light

Geocentric

An adjective used to describe a system of coordinates or orbits which are centred on the Earth. A description of the Solar System in which the Sun, Moon and planets are described as all moving around the Earth is a geocentric model.

Giant star

A star which belongs to a class of highly luminous stars which are exceptionally bright by virtue of their large size, in contrast with **dwarf** stars of a similar temperature. Many members of this class are red in colour, and are known as **red giants**.

See also: Hertzsprung-Russell diagram, spectral type, stellar evolution.

Globular cluster see star cluster

Globule

A small, dark **nebula** composed of opaque gas and dust.

Globules are detectable as small dark patches against the background of a rich star field or a cloud of glowing gas. They are often associated with the name of the American astronomer, Bart Bok, who first drew attention to them. They are comparatively small nebulae, with dimensions comparable with the size of the Solar System.

It is thought that globules may represent an early stage in star formation, when the material of a future star is consolidating under mutual gravitational attraction.

Granulation

The mottled appearance of the Sun's **photosphere** when viewed at high **resolution**.

Ideal conditions are needed for seeing the solar granulation. The mottled texture known as granulation then appears as a seething mass of bright patches of light, each about 1,000 km across, with a dark border. The pattern of granulation changes continuously, each cell lasting only a few minutes. The granulation may be picturesquely described as the boiling motion of the gas at the surface of the Sun.

Gravity

Gravity is one of the four natural forces of nature. It is the weakest of the four but acts over enormous distances. The force of gravity is perceived by humans as weight.

Physicists have discovered that four fundamental forces govern the behaviour of all matter. Two of these, the gravitational force and the electromagnetic force, are familiar in everyday life. The other two are encountered only within atoms and their nuclei. Of these four forces, the gravitational force was discovered first, by Isaac **Newton**. He consolidated the work of **Galileo** and **Kepler**, and developed a mathematical theory to account for a variety of apparently unrelated phenomena: the motion of bodies, the swing of a pendulum, and the orbit of the Moon. At the core of this theory lay the idea that massive bodies (that is, objects that have mass) exert a force on each other. For two bodies, the simplest case, the force is in direct proportion to the two masses and depends inversely on the square of the distance separating them. The force always attracts; it is, therefore, unlike a magnetic force where either attraction or repulsion may occur. Newton's discovery was that the ability to exert a force, that of gravity, was an innate property of massive objects. Gravity swings the pendulum, keeps the Moon in orbit, and makes apples fall from trees.

It is in astronomy that we encounter situations in which gravity is the dominant force because astronomical bodies (**planets, stars, galaxies**) have huge masses. Thus, the motion of the planets within the Solar System is governed entirely by the force of gravity exerted by the Sun and planets on each other. Similarly the stars of our **Galaxy** are kept together by the gravitational field of the Galaxy itself. The force of gravity prevents the Sun from exploding like a nuclear bomb.

In the early 20th century, Newton's theory of universal gravitation was superseded by Einstein's general theory of **relativity**, which attempts to explain the origin of the gravitational force.

H

Halley, Edmond

An English astronomer who lived from 1656 to 1742 and gave his name to the most famous of all periodic **comets**. He held the post of Astronomer Royal from 1720 to his death.

Halley noticed that the orbits of comets which had appeared in 1531, 1607 and 1682 were very similar. He applied **Newton**'s theory of **gravity** to demonstrate that these three appearances were in fact the same comet travelling in a very elongated ellipse which brought it close to the Earth about every 75 years. He went on to predict the next appearance for late 1758, a prediction which turned out to be entirely correct. The first recorded appearance of Halley's comet was in 240 B.C., and another well-known return occurred in A.D. 1066.

Among Halley's other achievements is the discovery of the **proper motion** of the stars: the tiny but real motion of the stars across the sky due to their velocities in space. Halley found this effect by comparing old star catalogues with those of his day. He also suggested a method of measuring the distance between the Earth and the Sun by observing a **transit** of Venus across the Sun, which was later used successfully.

Halo

(1) A term used in the general sense to mean any diffuse or nebulous region surrounding the main visible part of an astronomical body.

(2) In particular, the spherical region of space enclosing the **Galaxy**, within which the globular **star clusters** and other stars remaining from the early stages of the Galaxy's life are distributed.

Haro galaxy see galaxy

Heliocentric

Describing a system of coordinates or orbits centred on the Sun.

The heliocentric model of the Solar System gradually gained acceptance following the publication of **Copernicus'** *De Revolutionibus* in 1543, displacing the **geocentric** models which had been favoured previously.

Heliostat see coelostat

Hertzsprung-Russell diagram

A graph which displays the relationship between **spectral type** (or temperature or colour) and luminosity for a number of stars.

What has come to be known as the Hertzsprung-Russell diagram was first described by Henry Norris Russell in 1913. Later, it was recognised that the same ideas had been put forward at about the same time by Ejnar Hertzsprung.

A Hertzsprung-Russell diagram (or H-R diagram) is conventionally plotted with spectral type, or its equivalent, along the horizontal axis, with decreasing temperature towards the right and luminosity, or its equivalent, along the vertical axis. Any

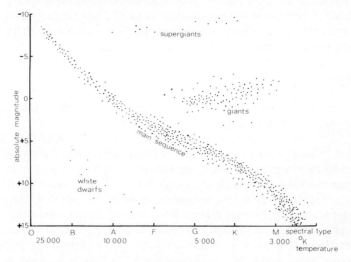

Fig. 12. A schematic Hertzsprung–Russell diagram, showing the location of the main sequence and the regions occupied by the giants, supergiants and white dwarfs.

star for which these two quantities are known may be plotted as a single point on the graph. However, the H-R diagram acquires most significance when the plotted points are restricted to a sample of stars which are related in some way, the members of a **star cluster** for example. The way the points are distributed in the diagram for a cluster gives an immediate visual indication of the cluster's age. The study of such diagrams has proved important in the development of the theory of **stellar evolution**.

Whatever sample of stars is chosen, it is found that the points on the H-R diagram are not distributed randomly. Most stars fall on a band running diagonally from the upper left to the lower right, termed the main sequence. The existence of the main sequence arises from the fact that a star's spectral type is governed predominantly by the mass of material it contains, which in turn relates also to the total intrinsic luminosity. The main sequence was once thought to be an evolutionary sequence. This is now known to be wrong. A star's position on the main sequence is dependent on its mass. The effects of evolution move stars away from the main sequence.

Above the main sequence, to the right, are the areas corresponding to the **giants** and **supergiants**. These huge evolved stars have luminosities far in excess of main sequence stars at the same temperature. Below the main sequence lie the **white dwarfs**, very under-luminous stars in a very late stage of evolution. Confusingly, the term "**dwarf**" is also applied to stars on the main sequence, particularly those at the lower end.

HII region

A region of space containing ionised hydrogen gas. Also written, more correctly, H^+ region.

A normal hydrogen atom consits of a positively charged proton which forms its nucleus, together with one negatively charged electron; the whole atom is electrically neutral. In the process of ionisation, the electrons are knocked off the atoms, and become separate free particles. The usual way that hydrogen becomes ionised in space is by the action of intense ultraviolet radiation from very hot stars. Gas clouds in which the hydrogen has become ionised generally have one or more luminous, hot stars buried inside them. The ionised hydrogen glows with a pinkish light. The HII region also emits infrared radiation and radio waves. These glowing clouds can be detected in distant

galaxies and their brightnesses used as a means of estimating the distances of the galaxies.

Among the many HII regions in our own **Galaxy**, the **Orion nebula** is the nearest, at a distance of about 500 **parsecs**.

Horsehead nebula

A famous dark nebula in the constellation of Orion, whose shape, clearly silhouetted against a background of glowing gas, bears some resemblance to a horse's head.

The area of nebulosity near the "belt" of Orion, of which the Horsehead forms a small part, contains both bright, glowing parts, and dark, opaque parts. The Horsehead is a small projection which protrudes from the dark area, in front of a bright area. It has become well-known largely because its unusual shape has made it a popular subject among astronomical photographs.

Hour angle

The length of **sidereal time** which has elapsed since an astronomical object last made a **transit** of the **meridian**.

As it takes 24 hours of sidereal time for the stars to complete a circle round the sky, angles around the **celestial sphere** can be measured in terms of the time it takes for the stars to sweep them out. 360° is equivalent to 24 hours, so 1 hour is 15°. The hour angle of an object is measured westwards form the meridian, and is usually given in units of hours, minutes and seconds of time.

Hubble's Law

A relationship, first proposed by Edwin Hubble, which states that the recession velocity of a **galaxy** is proportional to its distance from us.

The opening of the 100-inch Mount Wilson telescope in 1918 made it possible to measure the distances to nearby galaxies. Hubble discovered Cepheid **variable stars** in some of these galaxies and deduced their distances from the period-luminosity relation. In 1929 he published an astonishing discovery: the apparent recession velocities of galaxies were directly proportional to their distances. The constant linking the two is called Hubble's constant and its value is variously estimated today at

Fig. 13. The Horsehead, a well-known dark nebula clearly silhouetted against the bright glowing gas behind. (*Photograph from Kitt Peak National Observatory*)

between 50 and 100 kilometres per second per **megaparsec** of distance, about 10 times smaller than Hubble's original estimate.

The Hubble Law can be interpreted as evidence favouring the expansion of the universe from an initial **Big Bang**; although this is not the only feasible explanation it is currently the most convincing.

The reciprocal, or inverse, of Hubble's constant has the dimensions of time, and in some sense it can be considered as an estimate of the "age" of the universe, with a value of 20 billion years for a constant of 50 km/sec per megaparsec.

Hyades

An open **star cluster** in the constellation Taurus. The members appear to be scattered around the brightest star in Taurus, Aldebaran, which does not itself belong to the cluster. The brighter members of the Hyades are clearly visible to the naked eye. It is one of the most studied of all open clusters, and lies at a distance of about 150 light years.

I

I.C. abbreviation for Index Catalogue – see N.G.C.

Inferior conjunction see conjunction

Inferior planets

A collective term for the planets Mercury and Venus, whose orbits lie nearer to the Sun than the Earth's.

See Fig. 9, page 43.

Infrared astronomy

Study of the infrared radiation from cosmic bodies.

Infrared radiation is generally considered to cover the wavelength range from 800 nanometres to 1 millimetre, beyond which the radio region of the electromagnetic **spectrum** commences. Although it is possible to observe some infrared radiation at ground level, the absorption within our atmosphere as well as radiation it emits itself poses severe problems. The operational infrared telescopes are therefore at high altitudes, such as Mauna Kea in Hawaii at over 4,000 metres, where they are above most of the water vapour in the atmosphere. Infrared astronomy is also carried out from balloons and rocket observatories. In the early 1980s satellites will provide infrared astronomers with suitable facilities in space.

There are thousands of infrared sources within the **Milky Way**. Many of these are cool giant stars, which emit the bulk of their energy in the infrared. Also of great importance is the strong infrared source at the centre of the **Galaxy**, which may be emission either from dust that has been heated by hot stars or from electrons interacting with magnetic fields to produce synchrotron radiation.

Intergalactic medium

General term for any material which may exist isolated in space, far from **galaxies**.

It is not certain that any material at all lies between the galaxies, because such matter is very difficult to detect. Theoretical considerations suggest that material may exist between the galaxies. It is hard to believe, for example, that the formation of galaxies was so efficient that all the material in the **universe** is now to be found in the galaxies alone. Stronger arguments come from **cosmology**. At present the balance of evidence indicates that the universe is closed: it does not stretch to infinity in every direction. The amount of material needed to ensure that the universe is closed can be quite easily calculated. This quantity is about fifty times greater than the observable mass concentrated into galaxies. From this it might be concluded that the intergalactic medium has a far greater total mass than the combined mass of all galaxies. At the same time it is not difficult for this material, if it really does exist, to remain undetected by our telescopes. Observations of giant **radio galaxies** perhaps indicate an interaction between the radio-emitting clouds and the supposed medium outside the galaxies, but this evidence is not strong. The best pointer comes from **X-ray astronomy**: it has been found that **clusters of galaxies** are strong X-ray sources, on account of very hot gas permeating the intergalactic space within the cluster. In fact it makes up a significant fraction of the total cluster mass and may be material that has been captured from true intergalactic space.

Interstellar medium (or interstellar matter)

The matter which exists in the "space" between the stars.

Although interstellar space is nowhere totally empty, the density there is generally lower than in the best laboratory vacuum that can be produced on Earth. However, the sheer volume of space is so large that our own **Galaxy** contains in the region of 10^{10} solar masses of interstellar material. Most of it lies within the plane of the Galaxy. It consists primarily of the gases hydrogen and helium, together with small dust particles.

The presence of interstellar matter is obvious where **nebulae** are visible. Both bright glowing clouds of gas, such as the **Orion nebula**, and dark obscuring clouds, such as the **Coalsack**, are seen. In these clouds, the matter is much denser than in typical interstellar space.

The interstellar clouds are the sites of star formation. Very young stars, and stars still emerging from their parent gas clouds are often seen in regions of nebulosity. In a few clouds, notably one near the Galactic centre, called Sagittarius B2, numerous organic molecules, some quite complex, have been identified by means of their spectra in the radio region.

While young stars are appearing from interstellar matter, older stars are continually enriching the composition of the medium by material ejected into space. **Novae, supernovae** and **planetary nebulae** all blow off material from their outer layers, introducing fresh supplies of the elements heavier than hydrogen and helium into interstellar space. Our Galaxy, like all spiral galaxies, is fairly rich in interstellar material compared with ellipitical galaxies which are practically devoid of it.

See also: HII region.

Irregular galaxy see galaxy

Island universe

Formerly used as a popular term for a **galaxy**, when the discovery of galaxies beyond our own was still a comparative novelty.

J

Jupiter

The largest planet in the Sun's family, fifth in order of distance from the Sun.

Jupiter is one of the brightest objects in the night sky, reaching magnitude −2.5 when it is favourably placed. Its appearance is dominated by a pattern of light and dark bands running parallel to the equator. Spots of varying size also appear. The most well known is the Great Red Spot, first recorded over 300 years ago. These features move and change in size, position and colour.

Jupiter is noticeably flattened at its poles, this oblateness being due to the rapid rotation. The rotation period based on Jupiter's most stable features is 9.84 hours, but Jupiter is mainly gaseous, so different parts move at different rates.

In viewing the visible disc of Jupiter, we are seeing the top of thick cloud layers. The circulation and turbulent motion observed are analogous to weather patterns in the Earth's atmosphere. Much important information about Jupiter's atmosphere was gained by **Pioneer** 11, the American probe which passed close to Jupiter in 1974, and even greater detail was revealed by **Voyagers** 1 and 2 which encountered Jupiter in 1979. The Great Red Spot, for example, is a high pressure area in Jupiters weather system, a very long-lived anticyclone.

Jupiter is composed mainly of hydrogen with about 10 per cent helium, though ammonia and methane are prominent in its spectrum. There is so much material that Jupiter's core is compressed to solid, metal-like hydrogen. Jupiter is radiating more energy than it receives from the Sun, so it must have an internal source of heat. Possibly energy is released as the planet contracts under its own weight.

Jupiter has a strong magnetic field, and radiation belts which are similar to the **Van Allen** belts around the Earth, but far more intense, where electrically charged particles are trapped by the magnetic field. These particles contribute to Jupiter's radio

Fig. 14. Jupiter photographed by Voyager 1 in 1979 at a distance of 20 million miles (33 million kilometres). The Great Red Spot is the major feature to the south of the equator. Numerous other spots and detailed cloud structure can be seen. (*NASA photograph*)

emission, along with electrical discharges associated with the orbital motion of the moon, Io. Electrical activity was observed by the Voyager spacecraft in the form of aurorae and lightning.

Jupiter is accompanied by a family of at least 14 natural satellites, four of which are easily visible in a small telescope or binoculars. These Galilean moons are similar in size to our Moon or the planet Mercury. Most of the others are tiny, only some 10 or 20 km across, and are probably captured asteroids. The innermost moon, Amalthea, is some ten times larger than the rest, at 160 km in diameter, and Himalia, seventh in order from the planet, is 100 km in diameter.

In their 30,000 photographs the Voyagers returned a wealth

of unexpected detail about the Galilean moons. Perhaps the greatest surprise was the marked difference between them. Io is the only body in the solar system, apart from the Earth, known to have active volcanoes. Eight violent eruptions were witnessed. Its surface shows a diversity of light and dark colour, which is covered by sulphur and frozen sulphurous gases. Europa's surface is covered by a complex pattern of streaks which are probably fractures in a crust of ice, perhaps 100 km thick, overlying a rocky interior. There is little evidence of impact craters, or any kind of relief features.

Ganymede and Callisto have lower densities and probably have substantial crusts of ice and slush. Both show impact craters with rays and brighter white areas where fresh ice has been exposed. Callisto appears to be the most heavily cratered object so far discovered in the Solar System.

Voyager 1 also detected a faint ring in Jupiter's equatorial plane, similar in nature to Saturn's ring, but invisible from Earth. Estimates put the ring at 6,000 km wide and 1 km thick.

JUPITER'S MOONS

Number	Name	Diameter (km)	Mean Distance from Jupiter (km)	Orbital Period (days)
V	Amalthea	200	181,000	0.50
I	Io	3,652	422,000	1.77
II	Europa	2,900	671,000	3.55
III	Ganymede	5,273	1,070,000	7.15
IV	Callisto	4,500	1,883,000	16.69
XIII	Leda	(10)	11,110,000	239
VI	Himalia	100	11,480,000	250.6
X	Lysithea	(20)	11,710,000	259.2
VII	Elara	(30)	11,740,000	259.7
XII	Ananke	(20)	21,200,000	631
XI	Carme	(20)	22,600,000	692
VIII	Pasiphae	(20)	23,500,000	744
IX	Sinope	(20)	23,600,000	758
XIV	–	Yet to be confirmed		

See also: Solar System for table of planetary data.

K

Kepler, Johannes

The famous German astronomer who lived from 1571 to 1630, remembered chiefly for the three laws of planetary motion which he deduced.

Kepler was born in Wurtemberg, but he became assistant to the great Danish astronomer, **Tycho Brahe**. After Tycho's death, Kepler took over the vast amount of observational data that had been collected on the positions of the planets. He used this data to justify the **Copernican** model of the **Solar System**, in which all the planets orbit the Sun. In the course of this work, he discovered that the orbits of the planets are not circles, but are elliptical in shape. The Sun lies at one of the foci of the ellipse for each planet, and not at the centre. The distance between a planet and the Sun is thus variable, and Kepler found that the planets move more quickly when closer to the Sun, and slower when they are further away. The third law states that the squares of the sidereal periods of the planets are proportional to the cubes of their average distances from the Sun. **Sir Isaac Newton** later showed that these rules governing planetary motion are a natural consequence of the law of **gravitation**.

Kepler observed a **supernova** in the constellation Ophiuchus, in October 1604, which is sometimes called Kepler's star. Kepler also concerned himself with the mystical significance of the orbits of the planets, and he looked for relationships between them both in terms of the regular solid figures in geometry, and musical harmonies.

Kiloparsec see parsec

L

Libration

The variation in the part of the Moon's surface which is visible from the Earth.

The Moon rotates on its own axis in exactly the same time that it takes to complete an orbit around the Earth. The effect of this is that the Moon always keeps the same face turned towards the Earth. However, a number of phenomena contribute to a "wobble" which brings a total of 59 per cent of the Moon's surface into view at some time. Effects contributing to libration include the elliptical shape and the tilt of the Moon's orbit, and the different directions from which the Moon is viewed at different times of the day.

Light year

A unit of distance frequently used in popular astronomy, defined as the distance travelled by light in one year. As the speed of light is practically 300,000 km per second, a light year is equivalent to 9.46×10^{12} km. In professional astronomy the **parsec** is more commonly used, being about 3.26 light years.

Limb

The outermost edge of the visible disc of the Sun, the Moon or a planet.

The brightness of the visible **photosphere** of the Sun diminishes from the centre to the limb and the darkening around the edge of the disc is usually noticeable in photographs. This phenomenon is called limb darkening and is due to the fact that the photosphere is not completely opaque, and that there is a decrease in temperature towards the outer layers. In X-ray and radio emission from the Sun there is a limb brightening due to the hotter **chromosphere** and **corona** surrounding it.

Local Group

Name of the local cluster of **galaxies** to which the **Milky Way** system belongs.

Our Local Group of galaxies is fairly small compared to typical clusters in the universe. There are about two dozen members of this family of galaxies, although astronomers in the future may discover further faint galaxies in the Group. Its diameter is roughly five million light years. The Group is dominated by three large spiral galaxies: our **Galaxy**, the **Andromeda Nebula** (M31) and the Triangulum galaxy (M33). It is fortunate for astronomers that the Milky Way is part of a cluster of galaxies. Within the Local Group there are several different types of galaxy near at hand: giant spirals, dwarf elliptical galaxies, and irregular galaxies are all present to be compared and contrasted.

Luna program

The Soviet program of unmanned space probes for photographing and exploring the Moon.

Between 1959 and 1976, the Soviet Union sent 24 probes to the Moon, starting with attempts simply to crash land, but culminating in the successful use of remotely controlled vehicles and the return to Earth of samples of lunar rock.

In 1959 Luna 2 became the first space probe to reach the Moon's surface and was closely followed by Luna 3 which returned the first ever photographs of the back of the Moon. Luna 9 made a soft landing on the Moon in 1966, and sent back to Earth the first photographs from the Moon's surface. Luna 10 became the first artificial satellite to orbit the Moon, also in 1966. Luna 16 soft-landed in 1970, collected 100 grams of lunar soil and brought it safely back to Earth. Later in 1970 Luna 17 took an eight-wheeled vehicle, Lunokhod 1, which was a remotely controlled laboratory for lunar exploration. It operated for nearly a year during which time it covered a distance of about 10 kilometres. Luna 20 brought back more soil samples, and Luna 21 took Lunokhod 2 to the Moon in 1973. The final mission in the series, Luna 24, collected a 170g sample in 1976.

Lunar see eclipse, month, Moon, etc.

Lunation

One complete cycle of the **phases** of the Moon which takes one lunar **month** (synodic month), an interval of 29.53 days.

M

Maffei galaxy see galaxy

Magellanic Clouds

Two small **galaxies** visible in the southern hemisphere as faint patches of misty light.

The Magellanic Clouds are so named because the explorer Ferdinand Magellan was the first person to record sightings of them, in 1519. Both Clouds are visible to the naked eye as misty patches. In fact they are not clouds of gas, as the name might suggest, but dwarf galaxies situated about 180,000 light years beyond the **Milky Way**. Compared to normal spiral galaxies they are relatively small, containing a few billion stars and having diameters of about 30,000 light years. They are actually in orbit about our **Galaxy**.

Within the Magellanic Clouds there is an abundance of young stars; the Clouds also have much more interstellar gas, proportionally, than our Galaxy. Furthermore, stars in the Clouds are not identical, chemically, to stars in our Galaxy because the Clouds tend to be richer in heavier elements. For astrophysicists the Clouds are an extremely important area of study because all the stars within them are at essentially the same distance. Any differences among the stars must therefore be independent of distance. This is important because uncertainties as to the precise distances of individual stars in our own Galaxy make comparative studies difficult. We have a beautiful example of this from history. The properties of Cepheid **variable stars** were discovered by looking at Cepheids in the Clouds; the fact that all the Cepheids could be considered as being at the same distance made this discovery possible.

Magnetosphere

The region of space around the Earth, or around any other

planet having a magnetic field, which is dominated by the planet's own magnetic field.

A constant stream of electrically charged particles flows from the Sun out into the planetary system. When these particles encounter the magnetic field of a planet, they are deflected around the planet's sphere of magnetic influence, and they shape the field at the boundary of this sphere. On the side of the planet away from the Sun, there is a shadow where the charged particles cannot reach, and the magnetosphere has an extensive tail along this direction.

See Fig. 27, page 158.

Magnitude

A measure of the brightness of a star, or other astronomical object.

The magnitude system for describing the brightness of stars has been handed down from the Greek astronomer, Hipparchus. In 120 B.C. he tried to estimate the relative brightnesses of the stars, and became the first person to do so. He described the brightest stars which can be seen with the naked eye (as the telescope was not invented until much later, of course) as being of the "first magnitude", those somewhat dimmer as "second magnitude" and so on down to the "sixth magnitude" for the least conspicuous stars. The modern accurate definition of magnitude dates from about 1854 when Pogson showed that the magnitude steps represent brightness ratios: a first magnitude star is a hundred times brighter than a sixth magnitude star which in turn is a hundred times brighter than an eleventh magnitude star. A magnitude difference of one corresponds to a brightness ratio of 2.512, which is the fifth root of 100 ($\sqrt[5]{100}$). The scale is fixed by reference to a few standard stars.

The brighter the object, the smaller the magnitude number, so very bright objects have to be assigned negative magnitudes. The faintest magnitude which has been reached with the aid of telescopes and electronics is about 27th. The magnitude scale can be applied equally to objects other than stars.

The magnitude observed from Earth depends on both the intrinsic brightness and the distance of an object. It is called the apparent magnitude. The intrinsic brightness is measured in terms of absolute magnitude, which is defined as the magnitude an object would appear to have if it were at the arbitrary distance of 10 **parsecs**.

The measured magnitude of an object may differ according to the way the measurement was made, and the range of wavelength or colour taken into account. Visual magnitudes refer to observation by eye. Photographic magnitudes relate to the response of standard photographic emulsion which is chiefly in the blue and violet part of the spectrum. Bolometric magnitudes have corrections added so that they include the complete range of radiations, both visible and outside the visible region.

Some examples:

object	apparent magnitude	absolute magnitude
the Sun	−26.78	+4.71
the full Moon	−12.6	
Venus at its brightest	−4	
the brightest star, Sirius	−1.5	+1.41
Pole Star	+2.0	−4.5
the nearest star, Proxima Centauri	+10.7	+15.1
the faintest detectable galaxies	about +27	about −20
a very bright meteor	−5 to −10	

Main sequence see Hertzsprung-Russell diagram

Maksutov telescope

A reflecting **telescope** incorporating in its design a deeply curved lens, which corrects optical **aberrations** to give high quality images over a wide field of view.

The most commonly used practical arrangement is the **Cassegrain**-type system. An aluminised spot on the back of the corrector plate acts as a secondary mirror. The image is formed just behind the primary mirror, which has a small central hole. Difficulties in making large corrector plates limit the design to smaller apertures. The telescope is named after its Soviet designer.

Mariner program

A series of space probes launched by the United States in the 1960s and 70s some of which were sent to Mercury and Venus, the rest to Mars. None of the Mariner probes landed on any planet, but photography and physical measurements were carried out as the probes passed close to the planets.

SUCCESSFUL MARINER PROBES

Mariner No.	target	date	comments
2	Venus	1962	first successful fly-by
4	Mars	1965	first successful probe to Mars
5	Venus	1967	
6	Mars	1969	
7	Mars	1969	
9	Mars	1971	put into orbit around Mars
10	Venus & Mercury	1974	first two-planet mission

The Mariner program was astonishingly successful in returning high-quality photographs. It was Mariner 4 that revealed, for the first time, craters on Mars. Mariner 9 went into orbit around Mars, obtaining 7,329 photographs revealing a wealth of surface features. Mariner 10 exceeded all expectations; it made 3,500 photographs of Venus. Its orbit then allowed three separate encounters with Mercury which provided 10,000 pictures of its barren surface. The final probes, Mariner 11 and 12, were re-named **Voyager** 1 and 2 and aimed at the outer planets.

Markarian galaxy see galaxy

Mars

The fourth planet from the Sun in the Solar System, distinctly red in colour, even to the naked eye.

Although Mars is only a little over half the Earth's diameter, it is the most Earth-like planet in the Solar System. Like the Earth, Mars experiences seasons because its axis of rotation is tilted with respect to its orbit. There is an atmosphere, although the pressure is only 0.007 of that at the Earth's surface, and its composition is very different from our air, being 95 per cent carbon dioxide, with small quantities of nitrogen and other gases. Nevertheless, Mars experiences weather, including some

Fig. 15. A view across Mars, composed from four frames photographed by the Viking 1 Orbiter in 1976. Layers of haze in the Martian atmosphere can be seen over the horizon. (*NASA photograph*)

cloud and strong winds, but there is no free water to form rain or rivers.

Mars has only a weak magnetic field. This is probably because the planet's central core is small, whereas the Earth has a substantial iron-rich core. However, the surface rocks on Mars are rich in iron, giving it the characteristic rusty-red colour.

Mars is not an easy planet to observe telescopically. Although it is the nearest superior planet, its apparent disc is so small that it is difficult to distinguish surface features. Mars is best placed for observation at **opposition**. Because Mars' orbit is perceptibly elliptical, some oppositions bring it rather closer than others. The difficulties of observation led observers in the past to imagine features, such as the famous "canals", which are now known not to exist. The most conspicuous features are the white polar caps, and permanent darker areas on the rusty-red disc. Seasonal changes in the colouration are observed.

The true nature of the Martian surface was revealed first by the **Mariner** probes of the United States. Mariner 4 in 1965 was the first successful probe to Mars, which sent back photographs on its fly-by showing a cratered surface. Mariners 6 and 7 which flew by Mars in 1969, and Mariner 9 which entered orbit around Mars in 1971 provided extensive photographic coverage of Mars. Among the discoveries were several very large, extinct volcanoes. Olympus Mons, 600 km across and rising 25 km above the surrounding area, is the largest known volcano in the Solar System. There is also a giant canyon, called the Valles Marineris, which is 4,000 km long, 150 km and more wide, and 2 to 3 km deep.

The southern hemisphere of Mars is more heavily cratered than the northern hemisphere which, being at a slightly lower level, seems to have been flooded by volcanic lava since the time when most of the impact craters were created. What craters there are in the north are comparitively fresh looking, whereas many in the south are worn and eroded, as if by weathering. The high winds of Mars raise enormous dust storms which may engulf the whole planet. These global dust baths start when Mars is at **perihelion** and receiving maximum heat from the Sun.

The polar caps are thought to consist of small permanent caps of frozen water, with carbon dioxide frost which comes and goes with the seasons. There is no longer any running water on Mars, but sinuous channels in the equatorial region suggest that water once flowed on the surface, at a time when Mars' climate was rather milder than it is now.

In 1976 the **Viking** probes successfully soft-landed vehicles on the surface of Mars. It was already clear that no macroscopic forms of life are present on Mars. The Viking experiments to detect micro-organisms gave equivocal results.

Mars has two tiny natural satellites. They are both probably captured asteroids and have the appearance of pock-marked potatoes in photographs. Phobos is $20 \times 23 \times 28$ km in size and orbits Mars in 0.32 days. Deimos is $10 \times 12 \times 16$ km and has an orbital period of 1.26 days.

See also: Solar System for table of planetary data.

Maunder diagram see butterfly diagram

Megaparsec see parsec

Mercury

The planet nearest to the Sun.

Mercury is the smallest planet in the Solar System (with the possible exception of Pluto), with a diameter of 4,880 km. Its position, always close to the Sun in the sky, and small size have meant that little was known about the planet until **Mariner** 10 approached close in 1974 and returned photographs and physical data. Mercury's **elongation** never exceeds 28°. Even Mercury's axial rotation period was erroneously believed to be synchronous with its orbital period of 88 days, until 1965 when radar measurements showed the rotation period to be 59 days.

Much of Mercury's photographed surface is heavily cratered, and bears a strong resemblance to the Moon. As on the Moon there are also smoother areas which are probably lava flows, obliterating prior cratering. The distribution in crater size is somewhat different, though, probably because of Mercury's stronger gravity. Though small, Mercury has a large iron-rich core giving the planet a mean density close to the Earth's. Mercury also has a magnetic field, but only one hundredth the strength of the Earth's.

There is no atmosphere proper, though traces of helium and argon were found by Mariner 10. These gases probably originate in the rocks, from where they are replenished. Mercury is too small to retain much of an atmosphere, added to which the very high temperatures reached would cause any gases to boil off into space very rapidly. Maximum daytime temperatures reach 450 °C, but at night, the temperature falls as low as −180 °C.

See also: Solar System for table of data.

Meridian

On the **celestial sphere,** the circle which passes through the North and South Poles and the **zenith,** crossing an observer's horizon at points due north and south.

Another way of describing the meridian is the line of **right ascension** passing overhead. The right ascension of the meridian is the **sidereal time.**

See Fig. 3, page 18.

Messier's catalogue

A catalogue of 108 **galaxies, star clusters** and **nebulae,** originally drawn up by the French astronomer Charles Messier and published in 1770. The original list contained 45 objects, and this was supplemented later, with additional contributions from Messier's colleague, Pierre Mechain.

Messier's primary interest was searching for **comets,** but he noted down the positions of hazy objects which he observed during comet searches. He did not set out to make a systematic catalogue of nebulae. Nevertheless, he included most of the brighter galaxies, star clusters and gaseous nebulae, visible in the sky from Paris. Objects in his list are designated M1, M2, M3, etc, and these names are still in common use among amateur and professional astronomers.

MESSIER'S CATALOGUE

Messier No	description	constel-lation	other details
1	supernova remnant	Tau	Crab Nebula
2	globular cluster	Aqr	
3	globular cluster	CVn	
4	globular cluster	Sco	
5	globular cluster	Ser	
6	open cluster	Sco	
7	open cluster	Sco	

Messier No	description	constellation	other details
8	gaseous nebula	Sgr	Lagoon Nebula
9	globular cluster	Oph	
10	globular cluster	Oph	
11	open cluster	Sct	
12	globular cluster	Oph	
13	globular cluster	Her	
14	globular cluster	Oph	
15	globular cluster	Peg	
16	open cluster with nebulosity	Ser	
17	open cluster with nebulosity	Sgr	Omega or Horse-shoe Nebula
18	open cluster	Sgr	
19	globular cluster	Oph	
20	gaseous nebula	Sgr	Trifid Nebula
21	open cluster	Sgr	
22	globular cluster	Sgr	
23	open cluster	Sgr	
24	detached portion of Milky Way	Sgr	Not a true cluster
25	open cluster	Sgr	
26	open cluster	Sct	
27	planetary nebula	Vul	Dumbbell Nebula
28	globular cluster	Sgr	
29	open cluster	Cyg	
30	globular cluster	Cap	
31	spiral galaxy	And	"Great Nebula in Andromeda"
32	elliptical galaxy	And	companion of M31
33	spiral galaxy	Tri	seen face on
34	open cluster	Per	
35	open cluster	Gem	
36	open cluster	Aur	
37	open cluster	Aur	
38	open cluster	Aur	
39	open cluster	Cyg	
40	double star?	UMa	no satisfactory identification
41	open cluster	CMa	
42	gaseous nebula	Ori	Great Nebula in Orion

Messier No	description	constellation	other details
43	gaseous nebula	Ori	
44	open cluster	Cnc	
45	open cluster	Tau	Pleiades
46	open cluster	Pup	
47	open cluster	Pup	
48	open cluster	Hya	
49	elliptical galaxy	Vir	
50	open cluster	Mon	
51	spiral galaxy	CVn	Whirlpool galaxy
52	open cluster	Cas	
53	globular cluster	Com	
54	globular cluster	Sgr	
55	globular cluster	Sgr	
56	globular cluster	Lyr	
57	planetary nebula	Lyr	Ring Nebula
58	spiral galaxy	Vir	
59	elliptical galaxy	Vir	
60	elliptical galaxy	Vir	
61	spiral galaxy	Vir	
62	globular cluster	Oph	
63	spiral galaxy	CVn	
64	spiral galaxy	Com	
65	spiral galaxy	Leo	
66	spiral galaxy	Leo	
67	open cluster	Cnc	
68	globular cluster	Hya	
69	globular cluster	Sgr	
70	globular cluster	Sgr	
71	globular cluster	Sge	
72	globular cluster	Aqr	
73	group of four stars	Aqr	not a true cluster
74	spiral galaxy	Psc	
75	globular cluster	Sgr	
76	planetary nebula	Per	
77	Seyfert galaxy	Cet	
78	reflexion nebula	Ori	
79	globular cluster	Lep	
80	globular cluster	Sco	
81	spiral galaxy	UMa	
82	irregular galaxy	UMa	

Messier No	description	constel-lation	other details
83	spiral galaxy	Hya	
84	elliptical galaxy	Vir	
85	elliptical galaxy	Com	
86	elliptical galaxy	Vir	
87	peculiar galaxy	Vir	strong radio source
88	spiral galaxy	Com	
89	elliptical galaxy	Vir	
90	spiral galaxy	Vir	
91	spiral galaxy	Com	identification uncertain
92	globular cluster	Her	
93	open cluster	Pup	
94	spiral galaxy	CVn	
95	spiral galaxy	Leo	
96	spiral galaxy	Leo	
97	planetary nebula	UMa	Owl Nebula
98	spiral galaxy	Com	
99	spiral galaxy	Com	
100	spiral galaxy	Com	
101	spiral galaxy	UMa	
102			duplicate name of M101, through error
103	open cluster	Cas	
104	spiral galaxy	Vir	Sombrero galaxy
105	elliptical galaxy	Leo	
106	spiral galaxy	CVn	
107	globular cluster	Oph	
108	spiral galaxy	UMa	
109	spiral galaxy	UMa	
110	elliptical galaxy	And	companion of M31

Meteor

The momentary streak of light observed in the sky as a fragment of interplanetary material burns up through frictional heating in the upper atmosphere. Meteors are commonly called "shooting stars".

On a clear dark night, a few meteors can often be observed. These random meteors are described as sporadic. When the

Earth's orbital motion carries it through a region of space containing a concentration of interplanetary dust and debris, a meteor shower may occur. If the conditions are favourable, the frequency of observable meteors may reach hundreds in an hour, though a rather smaller rate is more usual, even in a shower. The shower meteors all appear to diverge from one point in the sky, called the radiant. This is a perspective effect, because all the meteors are entering the atmosphere from a single direction in space, as the Earth sweeps into the stream. Some meteor showers occur regularly every year, and last usually between a day and a week. The showers are named after the constellations in which their radiants lie. For example the Perseids come between July 25 and August 18, and the Geminids between December 7 and December 15.

Meteorite

Remnant of interplanetary matter which survives passage through the Earth's atmosphere, and falls to the surface.

Meteorites may be recognised either because they are seen to fall, or because of their characteristic structure and composition. A falling meteorite produces a brilliant **meteor** trail, known as a **fireball**. It is estimated that some 500 probably hit the Earth each year, but on average only half a dozen of those seen to fall are recovered, although ancient meteorites are frequently discovered. There are three main types: stony, iron and stony-iron. Many different minerals have been found in meteorites. The commonest are silicate rocks forming the stony element, and a mixture of iron and nickel. The minerals in meteorites are not the most abundant on Earth. The study of meteorites throws light on the origin of the Solar System and the chemical elements in it.

Stony meteorites can be divided into two groups: the chondrites which contain small spherical aggregates called chondrules, and the achondrites, from which chondrules are absent. Among the chondrites, a small number called carbonaceous chondrites are of particular interest because of their unusual composition, which includes organic compounds. Chondrites are thought to represent fairly closely the composition of the material from which the **Solar System** formed, except for the lightest elements which escape easily into space.

Large meteorites may weigh many tonnes, and the impact of

such a meteorite leaves a substantial crater, such as the famous Barringer crater in the Arizona desert. Weathering on Earth has long since destroyed any evidence of meteoric impact in the remote past, but the cratered surfaces of many other bodies in the Solar System, such as the Moon and Mercury, show that meteorites must have been very abundant in the early Solar System.

Meteorites were probably manufactured as a result of collisions in the asteroid belt, for their composition is very similar to the **asteroids**. It is probably that collisions between the Earth and very large meteorites are responsible for **tektites**. The number of meteorites available for study by scientists has recently greatly increased: ancient meteorites are strewn about abundantly on the ice shelf in Antarctica, where they may simply be picked up.

Microwave background radiation

The weak radio signal at microwave frequencies that can be detected with the same intensity from all parts of the sky.

The discovery of the cosmic background radiation in 1965 created a sensation, particularly among cosmologists. The signal is weak and is characteristic of radiation from an object having a temperature a mere 2.7 degrees above absolute zero. That object is the **universe** itself. The background has almost the same intensity in every direction, the very slight asymmetry being due to the motion of our **Galaxy** relative to the radiation.

It is generally considered that the background radiation is a relic of the early hot phase of the **Big Bang** universe. Today the universe has expanded considerably, and this expansion has lowered the temperature of the background to about 3°. The moment of its discovery was also a time of great controversy in **cosmology**, and this event tipped the balance very much in favour of the Big Bang model.

Far out in the universe, deep in the space between **clusters of galaxies**, the microwave background is the main source of radiation.

Milky Way

A band of hazy light forming a complete circle around the sky which results from the combined light from myriads of faint and distant stars in our own **Galaxy**.

The term Milky Way is sometimes used to mean our Galaxy as such, though strictly it should be applied to the belt of faint light which is our inside view of the Galaxy. Since the Galaxy resembles a disc with a central bulge in shape, from within it appears to be a belt all round. The light is much more intense towards the galactic centre in Sagittarius then it is in the outward direction, particularly as the Sun is situated towards the outer edge of the main disc of the galaxy. Even a small telescope or binoculars will resolve the Milky Way into stars. The difference in star density within the Milky Way, as compared with regions outside, is very noticeable. The plane of the Galaxy contains opaque dust and gas, as well as stars, which gives the Milky Way a patchy appearance. One well-known dark nebula within the Milky Way, near the Southern Cross, is the Coalsack.

The chief constellations through which the Milky Way passes are Perseus, Cassiopeia, Cygnus, Aquila, Sagittarius, Scorpius, Centaurus, Vela, Puppis, Monoceros, Orion, Taurus and Auriga.

Minor planet see asteroid

Month

The time which the Moon takes to orbit the Earth, relative to some point of reference.

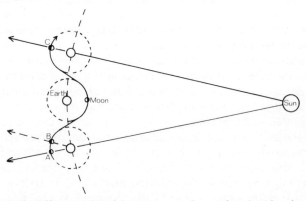

Fig. 16. The difference in length between a synodic month and a sidereal month arises because of the Earth's orbital motion around the Sun. At A and C the Moon has the same phase. At B and C the Moon has nearly the same position in the sky. The Moon takes about two days to travel from A to B.

The motion of the Moon is complex in detail and it is possible to define the month in a number of different ways, each giving a slightly different period. However, the two basic definitions which are of interest are: the time taken to complete a circuit of the sky relative to the stars, called the sidereal month; and the interval of time between successive new moons, called the synodic month. The sidereal month is 27.322 days and the synodic month 29.531 days. The difference arises because the Moon's **phase** depends also on the motion of the Earth around the Sun. During a sidereal month, the Earth travels along one-thirteenth of its orbit. It takes the Moon an extra two days to return to a point in its orbit where its phase is apparently the same again.

Moon

Earth's only natural satellite.

Apart from the Earth itself, the Moon has been the subject of more study and attention than any other astronomical object and is the only body to have been visited by men. It is the Earth's closest neighbour in space, at an average distance of 382 thousand kilometres, and has a diameter of 3,476 km which is about a quarter of the Earth's size. The Moon is less dense than Earth. Its mean density is 3.3 times that of water, compared with a figure of 5.5 for the Earth. The lower density and smaller size combine to give the Moon a mass only 0.012 times the Earth's mass.

The Moon orbits the Earth in 27.32 days, relative to the stars, going through the familiar cycle of phases during the course of the **month**. The interval between successive new moons is 29.53 days, since the Earth-Moon system is also in orbit around the Sun. The Moon rotates on its own axis in a period of a month, so that the same face is always presented to the Earth, except for the small effects of **libration**.

The Moon's orbit is inclined at about 5° to the plane of the **ecliptic**, so the Moon's path in the sky keeps close to the **zodiac** band. When the relative positions of the Moon, Sun and Earth are suitable, an **eclipse** of the Moon may occur. In eclipse, the Moon does not disappear completely, but takes on a reddish hue from light scattered by the Earth's atmosphere.

Even to the naked eye, it is clear that the Moon's surface has a variety of features. The darker areas are termed maria (meaning

Fig. 17. The Moon shown as a composite photograph of two half-moons. This technique shows up more surface detail than a real photograph of the full Moon, because the illumination of all the features is at an angle rather than direct. The dark, comparatively uncratered maria stand out in contrast to the more rugged, heavily cratered terrain. (*Lick Observatory photograph*)

"seas") though it has been known for a long time that there is no water on the Moon. In contrast there are brighter, more rugged areas which are mountainous and much more heavily cratered than the maria.

There are craters of all sizes. Some are overlapping, some have central mountains and some occur in chains. The vast majority were created by the impacts of **meteorites** which were much more abundant in the early days of the Solar System than they are now. A few craters are the result of volcanoes, but these tend to be smaller and more irregular. Volcanic activity did, however, produce one major feature, the maria. Large basins excavated by the impact of huge meteorites were then later filled in by flowing lava. Some craters, especially younger ones, are surrounded by circular areas of brighter material, and rays radiating outward. These are the result of debris thrown out from the initial impact, and secondary cratering.

Other features resulting from vulcanism include domes which rise gently in the ground in border regions of the maria and in the floors of some large craters, sinuous ridges extending for hundreds of kilometres across the maria and curving rilles, which are old lava channels.

The lunar farside has abundant cratering but no major maria, though there are some large basins where the filling by lava has been much less than on the nearside. The difference may be due to the thinner crust on the nearside, or perhaps the gravitational influence of the Earth.

Altogether 386 kilograms of lunar rock were brought back by the **Apollo** missions of the United States. Moon rocks are broadly similar to Earth rocks, though chemically distinctive, suggesting that the Moon had a separate origin. An interesting component found in the lunar soil is small glass "marbles", created in the heat of meteoric impact.

The Moon has a comparatively thick, immobile crust to a depth of between 30 and 100 kilometres. No movement takes place, so unlike on Earth there are no mountains formed by folding. There are some fault lines, leading to features such as the Straight Wall, and straight rilles. Under the lunar crust, there is a thick solid mantle, and a partly molten core. The exact composition of the core is unknown. It may possibly contain some iron, but the absence of a magnetic field suggests there is no large metallic core. See Fig. 20, page 104.

See also: phase, transient lunar phenomenon.

Morning Star

Applied to the planet Venus when it can be seen as a bright object in the eastern sky, just before sunrise. The planet Mercury is also described as being "a morning star" when visible before sunrise.

Mercury and Venus never get far from the Sun in the sky because their orbits lie inside the Earth's. Thus, they are observable either in the morning or evening, just before or just after sunrise when they are close to greatest western or eastern **elongation**. Mercury is fainter than Venus and nearer the Sun, and so it is a difficult planet to spot. The great brilliancy of Venus, especially noticeable in a twilit sky, when most stars are invisible, has led to the description "Morning Star" and "Evening Star".

N

Nadir

The point on the **celestial sphere** which lies directly below the observer, opposite the **zenith**. The nadir is thus a point below the horizon and cannot be observed.

Nebula

Literally meaning "cloud", the term nebula has been applied to any objects in the sky appearing hazy, rather than having sharp stellar images. It is now properly reserved for true clouds of interstellar gas and dust.

Nebulae may be either bright or dark. Bright nebulae can either emit light of their own, stimulated by radiation from hot stars within them, or they may simply reflect the light of a nearby star. Dark nebulae of opaque gas or dust are usually detected against the background of a bright nebula or star field.

Galaxies are still occasionally called extragalactic nebulae. Many objects formerly described as nebulae are now known to be star clusters. **Planetary nebulae** are evolved stars surrounded by a spherical shell of gas.

See also: interstellar medium.

Neptune

The eighth major planet of the Solar System.

Neptune is very similar to **Uranus**, showing a small greenish disc in a telescope. It never exceeds 7.7 magnitude in brightness, and is thus never visible to the naked eye. It was discovered in 1846 by J. G. Galle of the Berlin Observatory. Its existence had been predicted from the effect of its gravitational pull on the expected motion of Uranus, by Leverrier in France, and by the Englishman John Couch Adams.

Neptune has two known satellites, Triton and Nereid. Triton's motion is retrograde; that is, in the opposite direction to normal. A possible explanation is that Triton is a captured asteroid, or that Triton was sent into its unusual orbit by an event that ejected Pluto out of an orbit round Neptune, into its present situation.

See also: Solar System for table of planetary data.

Neutrino astronomy

Term applied to attempts to detect the neutrinos being emitted by our **Sun**.

The neutrino is one of the numerous fundamental particles that make atomic matter, and its existence was predicted in the 1930s. It has bizarre properties: at rest it would weigh nothing and it has no electric charge. Neutrinos travel at the speed of light, carry energy, and have almost no interaction with normal (everyday) matter. This last property makes it exceedingly difficult to detect (i.e. to capture) a neutrino. Their importance to astronomy stems from the fact that the nuclear reactor at the centre of the Sun should be an abundant source of neutrinos if our ideas about how the Sun works are correct. These solar neutrinos stream out of the nuclear core and flow almost unimpeded into space. Even by the time they encounter the Earth, a million million pass through an area the size of a large postage stamp every second.

An experiment to detect these neutrinos started in 1955, and an improved version is still in operation. Raymond Davis of the Brookhaven Laboratory has set up a "neutriono telescope" in part of a gold mine; it needs to be deep underground to avoid the detector being triggered by cosmic rays. The detector is 450,000 litres of perchloroethylene; one neutrino can cause one atom of chlorine in this fluid to turn into an atom of argon, although the probability of this is exceeding small.

The solar neutrinos experiment is, in fact, detecting only one-third of the neutrinos predicted from theory, and the origin of this discrepancy is unknown. It has been suggested by some theorists that the Sun's core may have a lower temperature than is indicated from current theories. If this is correct then the Sun's temperature may well fluctuate within narrow limits, giving a plausible explanation of the occurrence of major ice ages on the Earth.

Neutron star

A tiny star, a million million times denser than the Sun, which is made of neutrons.

Neutrons were discovered in 1932, and astro-physicists realised almost immediately that it was theoretically possible for dense stars composed primarily of neutrons to exist. By 1939 it was speculated that they might be made during the final collapse of the central part of an exploding star (i.e. **supernova**).

The discovery of **pulsars** (1967), particularly the one in the **Crab Nebula**, showed that neutron stars do indeed exist. They have masses in the range 1-2 solar masses and diameters of about 30 km. The inward gravitation crush for such a tiny star is indeed stupendous, but it is resisted by forces between the neutrons. These particles are formed during the gravitational collapse of the core of a dying star, as electrons and protons are forced to combine.

The final result of the evolution of stars that are less massive than neutron stars are **white dwarfs**, whereas objects that are too massive for neutron pressure to be effective presumably shrink down into **black holes**.

New General Catalogue see N.G.C.

Newton, Sir Isaac

English mathematician and scientist who lived from 1642 to 1729 and made numerous fundamental contributions to physics and astronomy.

Newton's most famous achievement is perhaps his formulation of the Universal Law of Gravitation. **Gravity** is the force which governs the motion of the planets in the solar system, and Newton was able to show how **Kepler**'s Laws of planetary motion are a natural consequence of the nature of gravity. He also made contributions to the study of optics and constructed the first practical reflecting **telescope**.

See also: Newtonian telescope.

Newtonian telescope

A reflecting **telescope** in which the light is brought to a focus at one side of the tube by means of a small flat mirror.

The Newtonian reflector was the original design for a reflecting telescope made by Sir Isaac **Newton**, and is still popular as an optical arrangement in small amateur instruments. It has the advantage of requiring only a single flat secondary mirror, and does not require a hole in the centre of the primary mirror.

See Fig. 26, page 149.

N.G.C.

An abbreviation for New General Catalogue, prefixed before the numbers of objects in the catalogue when used as a means of identification. The catalogue, originally drawn up in 1888, listed the positions of all known nebulous objects, a total of over 7,000. Some of these objects have since been identified as **star clusters** or **galaxies**, rather than gaseous nebulae. The brightest ones also appear in **Messier's** catalogue. Supplements to the N.G.C., known as the Index Catalogues (I.C.) brought the total number of listed objects to over 13,000.

Northern lights see aurora

Nova

The sudden brightening of a star in an advanced state of evolution by as much as 18 **magnitudes**. The outburst is connected with the star's membership of a **binary system**.

Ordinary novae are subject to a single outburst, but some, called recurrent novae, suffer more than one eruption. A distinct group, called dwarf novae, also erupt repeatedly, but do not brighten by so large a factor as ordinary novae. The rise to maximum takes place rapidly, only a matter of hours or days. The nova lasts for a few days before a rapid decline, followed by a slower dimming, back to its former state. Because novae are unpredictable, amateur astronomers play an important role in their discovery.

During the eruption, a shell of gas is blown off the star. This activity is revealed by changes in the nova's **spectrum**. Dwarf novae increase in brightness by between 2 and 5 magnitudes at approximately regular intervals, of the order of tens or hundreds of days.

It has been shown that all novae are members of close binary systems. The tidal interaction between the stars causes gas to be transferred between the two and this triggers the outburst in an evolved star where the situation is already unstable. It seems likely that the evolved star is a **white dwarf**, and matter streams onto it from a cool companion star.

N-type galaxy see galaxy

Nubeculae Major and Minor see Magellanic Clouds

Nucleosynthesis

The creation of chemical elements in nuclear reactions which occur naturally, inside **stars** for example.

There are nearly one hundred naturally-occurring, stable, chemical elements, which are found in varying amounts. The two lightest, the gases hydrogen and helium, are by far the most abundant in the universe, together accounting for about 98 per cent of the mass. These elements probably date from soon after the creation of the universe, but it is thought that all the heavier elements have been produced subsequently as a result of nuclear reactions. The source of stellar energy is the fusion reactions in stellar interiors which transmute hydrogen into helium and heavier elements. It seems likely that nuclear reactions also take place when a star explodes as a **supernova**. Stellar interiors and supernova explosions are thus two examples of astrophysical situations where nucleosynthesis takes place.

Nutation see precession

O

Objective

The main lens in a refracting **telescope**, which collects the light from objects being observed and brings that light to a focus. The focused image is then viewed with an eyepiece.

An objective prism is a large thin prism, designed to be placed at the front of a telescope so that all the images in the field of view appear as small **spectra**.

Occultation

The hiding of one astronomical body by another, which passes in front of it as seen from a particular direction.

Occultations of stars by the Moon and planets occur frequently. It is also possible for the Moon to occult planets, or the planets each other. The moons of the other planets may also be occulted, when they are hidden behind the disc of their planet.

At any time the position of the Moon is known with very great precision. Therefore the observations of lunar occultations are important, because they provide a very accurate check on the positions of members of the **Solar System**, and can be used to gain information about the atmospheres of planets, or the position, dimensions and structure of such diverse objects as **asteroids** or radio sources.

There is some confusion between the terms occultation and **eclipse**. Strictly, an eclipse of the Sun is an occultation since the Sun is hidden directly behind the Moon.

Olbers' Paradox

The apparent difficulty in reconciling the darkness of the night sky, with an infinite universe of stars.

If the **universe** were infinite in extent, unchanging and filled with stars (or galaxies), then any line of sight out into space would ultimately end on a star, no matter how far away. In other words, the night sky would be as bright as a star all over! This is clearly not the case, and present-day understanding of the universe shows that there is no paradox. The universe is expanding and evolving. Radiation reaching us from the furthest reaches of space is so severely redshifted that the level of background radiation in the visible region is very low, and hence the sky is dark at night.

Open cluster see star cluster

Opposition

The position of the Moon or of a superior planet, when it is directly opposite the Sun in the sky.

The Moon is full at opposition, and reaches its highest point in the sky at midnight. The same is true for the **superior planets**. At opposition they are at their closest approaches to the Earth. As the orbits of the planets are elliptical, rather than perfectly circular, some oppositions bring the planets closer to Earth than others. In particular, Mars sometimes has very favourable oppositions.

At opposition, the **elongation** of the Moon or planet, that is, its angular distance from the Sun, is 180°.

See Fig. 9, page 43 and Fig. 10, page 44.

Orbiter program

A series of five American space probes placed in orbit around the Moon, to photograph the surface with a view to finding suitable landing sites for the **Apollo program**.

All five Orbiters, launched in 1966 and 1967, were successful, and together secured a photographic record of almost the entire lunar surface.

Orion Nebula

A glowing cloud of ionised hydrogen gas, visible to the naked eye as a fuzzy patch in Orion's Sword.

Long exposure photographs show the nebula as a beautiful series of wisps and loops glowing with the red light of hydrogen.

Fig. 18. The Orion Nebula, a cloud of glowing gas, visible to the naked eye as a faint misty patch in the "sword" of the constellation Orion. (*Lick Observatory photograph*)

At the centre of the nebula is a small group of very hot stars, known as the Trapezium, and it is the intense ultraviolet light from these that causes the glow of the nebula, by ionising the hydrogen. The nebula is about 1,800 light years away, and yet it is the nearest large **HII region**. Its diameter is roughly 20 light years.

Behind the nebula radio astronomers have discovered a giant molecular cloud containing many different types of molecule, and with a mass about 500 times that of our Sun. The central part of the molecular cloud is also a strong infrared source. It is very likely that this radiation is coming from active regions of star formation, as parts of the molecular cloud condense under the force of gravity to form new stars. In fact the molecular cloud in the Orion Nebula, and the **globules** seen in front of the glowing cloud, are the nearest sites of star formation. In 1936 a new star flared up in the Orion Nebula, giving a dramatic demonstration that this is indeed a birthplace of stars.

Orrery

A working model of the **Solar System** showing the planets, possibly with some of their moons, in their orbits around the Sun.

The term "orrery" was first applied to such a model in 1713, when one was made for the Fourth Earl of Cork and Orrery. These miniature planetary systems usually contain gear systems so that the orbital periods of the planets around the Sun are in the correct proportions. However, it is impossible to construct a model in which the distance scale is also correct, since the real distances between the planets are vast compared with the sizes of the planets themselves.

P

Parallax

The apparent shift in the relative positions of objects at different distances from an observer as that observer changes the angle from which he views them. In astronomy, the parallax of an object is used synonymously with its distance.

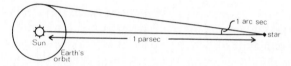

Fig. 19. The radius of the Earth's orbit is taken as the baseline for the measurement of a star's parallax angle. The parsec is a unit of distance defined as the distance an object would have if its parallax angle were one second of arc.

The measurement of angles of parallax is one of the main ways in which comparatively small distances on the astronomical scale are determined. Such a measurement requires a baseline of known size. Then trigonometry can be used to deduce the distance. The lunar and solar parallaxes can be measured by taking the radius of the Earth as a baseline. The radius of the Earth's orbit is used for determining the parallaxes of those stars near enough to show a detectable shift in position over a six-month period.

Parallax is measured in seconds of arc. Even the nearest star has a parallax of only 0.76 arc second, corresponding to a distance of just over four **light years**. A hypothetical object with a parallax of 1 arc sec is said to be at a distance of 1 parsec (abbreviated pc). The smaller the parallax, the greater the distance. Parallax angle p, and distance d, in parsecs are related simply by $d = 1/p$, so the parsec (equal to 3.26 light years) is a commonly used measure of distance in astronomy.

Even distances which have not been measured directly from parallax angles, but have been deduced from indirect observation, are often called parallaxes. For example, spectroscopic parallaxes are deduced by comparing the observed brightness of a star with its theoretical, intrinsic brightness, predicted from its **spectrum.**

Parsec

A unit of distance used in astronomy, equivalent to 3.26 **light years** or 30.86 × 10^{12} km.

The parsec (pc) is derived from distance measurements made by means of **parallax** angles and is the distance at which an object would show a parallax of 1 second of arc. For large distances the kiloparsec (kpc) and megaparsec (mpc), equal to one thousand and one million parsecs, may be used.

See Fig. 19, page 102.

Perihelion

The point in the orbit of a planet, comet, or other body which is closest to the Sun. The Earth is at perihelion on about January 3. (It is therefore closest to the Sun during the winter in the northern hemisphere.)

Phase

A description of the part and proportion of the disc of a planet or the Moon, which is visible by means of reflected sunlight. Phase, as observed from the Earth, is governed by the relative positions of the Earth, the Sun and the body in question.

The Moon undergoes a complete cycle of phases during the course of a synodic month. The cycle begins with new Moon, when the Moon lies between the Earth and the Sun, and its illuminated half is invisible from the Earth. Between new Moon and first quarter, the visible part of the Moon is a waxing crescent. Between first quarter, when the Moon appears as a semi-circle, and full Moon, the shape is described as gibbous. As the Moon wanes again, the phases are repeated in reverse, passing through third quarter at half Moon. The term "quarter" refers to the fact that the Moon is a quarter the way from the start or finish of its cycle of phases, or possibly that a quarter of the Moon's entire surface is visible, though this constitutes only half its visible disc.

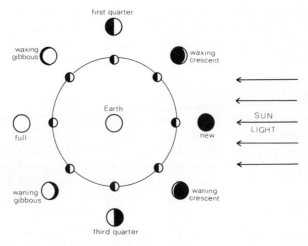

Fig. 20. The phases of the Moon. The fraction of the illuminated side of the Moon visible from the Earth varies as the Moon moves around the Earth.

More precisely, phase may be expressed in terms of the phase angle, which is defined as the angle between the two lines, planet (or Moon) to Sun, and planet (or Moon) to Earth.

The planets also exhibit phases. Mercury and Venus can be seen to go through a complete cycle of phases similar to the Moon's, because their orbits lie inside the Earth's. The **superior planets** are seen in gibbous phase, except at exact **opposition** when they are full. The more distant a planet, the more nearly full it appears for most of the time.

For superior planets, the phase angle, in degrees, divided by 180, gives the fraction of the hemisphere facing the Earth that is in darkness. It is greatest at **quadrature**.

Photometry

The accurate, quantitative measurement of the amount of light energy received from stars or other objects, as compared with standards.

Accurate photometry requires the careful use of standard equipment, such as photographic plates, or photoelectric devices, usually combined with filters, if the results are to be of value in comparing one star with another. Photometry also demands the best observing conditions since it is very difficult to correct for the absorption in hazy skies. Photometric systems have been devised in which stellar **magnitudes** are measured in certain restricted wavelength bands defined by standard filters. One of the most commonly encountered is the U.B.V. system, where the initials stand for ultraviolet, blue and visual.

Photosphere

The yellow surface layer of the **Sun**.

The photosphere is a layer about 500 kilometres thick. Within this zone the solar material makes the gradual transition from being completely opaque to light (the interior) and completely transparent (the **chromosphere** and lower **corona**). This, then, is the layer that actually emits the bulk of the heat and light that leave the Sun. The relative thinness of the photosphere, as compared to the solar diameter, accounts for the sharply-defined visible disc of the Sun. Within the photosphere the temperature is about 6,000 °K, at the lowest level falling to 4,000 °K at the base of the chromosphere. **Sunspots** are located in the photosphere. The **Fraunhofer lines** in the solar **spectrum** originate in the photosphere.

Pioneer program

A series of space probes launched by the United States of America for various investigations in the Solar System.

The series began in 1958 with efforts to send probes to the Moon which were unsuccessful. Pioneers 4 to 9 were placed in orbits around the Sun, and were used to monitor solar activity, especially during the manned **Apollo** flights, when additional solar radiation would have been hazardous. Pioneers 10 and 11 were directed towards Jupiter. In 1973 Pioneer 10 sent back the first close-up pictures of Jupiter. Pioneer 11 reached Jupiter in 1974 and Saturn in 1979, though the images of Saturn proved a disappointment.

The name Pioneer was also given to two probes to Venus launched in 1978. Pioneer Venus 1 orbited Venus and carried out radar mapping and other physical measurements. Pioneer Venus 2 released four secondary probes into Venus' atmosphere, one of which continued to transmit data after landing on the planet's surface.

Planet

One of the basically solid, non-luminous bodies in orbit about the Sun, or other similar bodies which may orbit other stars.

Planets shine only by the sunlight they reflect. There are nine known major planets: **Mercury, Venus, Earth, Mars, Jupiter, Saturn, Uranus, Neptune** and **Pluto**, together with large numbers of minor planets (**asteroids**). The word "planet" is derived from the Greek meaning "wanderer" since the paths of the planets appear to meander through the fixed pattern of **constellations**.

The structure of the planets varies one from another. The smaller planets are rocky, some with metal-rich cores. The giant planets, Jupiter, Saturn, Uranus and Neptune, have low densities, being for the most part fluid, with cores solidified by the huge pressure of material overlying them. There is a clear distinction between the planets and **comets**, which are much more diffuse collections of matter containing little mass.

The mechanism of planet formation is still uncertain. In our system they condensed from the same gas cloud (the so-called solar nebula) as did our Sun, but the precise way in which this happened is still unclear. It was once supposed that planets could be formed in a close encounter with another star, in which a stream of material would be plucked from the Sun and left stranded in space; this is definitely impossible.

No planet orbiting any other star has ever been observed directly, but irregularities in the motion of some nearby stars have led to the supposition that the gravitational effects of planets orbiting these stars may be responsible.

See also: under individual planets, and Solar System.

Planetarium

A special projector which produces spots of light on an overhead dome, resembling the pattern of stars and planets in the night sky. Planetarium is also used to describe the entire building in which such a projector is housed.

A good planetarium can give a startling impression of a real night sky. The projector is driven by motors which simulate the apparent motion of the stars and planets. This motion may be accelerated, or reversed to show the appearance of the sky on any date. The tilt of the projector may also be changed to give the viewer the impression of being at any chosen latitude on the Earth. Planetaria are used for teaching purposes and as a form of entertainment.

The term "planetarium" has been used in the past, and is still used sometimes for any model showing the stars and/or planets.

Planetary nebula

A shell of glowing gas surrounding an evolved star, from which it was ejected. Planetary nebulae are in no way related to planets. The misleading name arose from the visual resemblance between them and the disc of a planet, as viewed in a small telescope.

Planetary nebulae are composed chiefly of hydrogen which is ionised by the action of the radiation from the central star. The shells of gas are expanding. The appearance is often that of a ring, as in the case of the famous "Ring Nebula" in Lyra. Others resemble a dumbbell in shape.

Fig. 21. The Dumbbell, a planetary nebula in the constellation Vulpecula. *(Lick Observatory photograph)*

It is generally believed that planetary nebulae represent a late stage in the evolution of single stars with masses between one and four solar masses. An unstable situation during the **red giant** stage may lead to the ejection of the outer layers, leaving a hot core which has spent all its nuclear fuel. The exposed core is essentially a **white dwarf** which will slowly cool down until it no longer glows. Meanwhile, the shell of gas will diffuse into space.

See also: stellar evolution.

Pleiades

An open **cluster** of young stars in the constellation of Taurus, easily visible to the naked eye.

The familiar name for the Pleiades is the "Seven Sisters", but only six bright stars are visible to the naked eye. These are Alcyone, Maia, Atlas, Electra, Merope and Taygete. A small telescope or binoculars reveals many more stars. The cluster may contain as many as 3,000. The stars are surrounded by nebulosity which glows by reflexion from the stars. This is one of the youngest clusters, being about 20 million years old. Long exposure photographs reveal the delicate veils of gas near the stars, vestiges of the gas cloud from which the cluster itself condensed.

Plough

A familiar pattern of seven bright stars forming part of the constellation Ursa Major (the Great Bear).

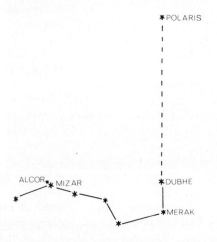

Fig. 22. The seven stars that form the Plough (Big Dipper) are part of the constellation Ursa Major (Great Bear). The stars Merak and Dubhe make a line which points to the Pole Star, Polaris. Alcor and Mizar form a double star system visible to the naked eye.

The Plough is a conspicuous formation in the northern part of the sky; it is not itself a **constellation**. From the temperate northern latitudes, the Plough is **circumpolar**. The two stars Dubhe and Merak are called the pointers because they make a straight line with the **Pole Star**. Other common names for the Plough are the Big Dipper, as the shape bears some resemblance to a ladle, and Charles' Wain – a wain being a cart.

Pluto

The ninth planet from the Sun in the **Solar System**.

Pluto is a small distant planet whose brightness never exceeds 14th **magnitude**, and therefore little is known about it. The discovery made in 1978 that Pluto has a moon (provisionally named Charon) has provided more accurate data on the size and mass of the planet than was known previously. Charon shows up only as a bulge in the apparent disc of Pluto in high resolution photographs, and it cannot be resolved separately. Its regular motion around Pluto revealed that a moon was really present. The best estimate for Pluto's mass is only 0.0026 Earth masses and for its diameter about 3,000 km, less than the size of our Moon. Charon appears to have about one tenth the mass of Pluto, and travels around its primary in an orbit of radius 20,000 km taking 6 days 9 hours to do so. Pluto has long been observed to vary in brightness fairly regularly with this period. It had been thought that patchiness on Pluto's surface was responsible, the total brightness changing as Pluto rotated. It seems likely that this may indeed be a contributing factor, and that Pluto's rotation period is synchronised with Charon's orbital period. Charon's orbit is virtually at right angles to Pluto's orbit around the Sun. If Charon's orbit in fact coincides with Pluto's equator as is likely, then Pluto's rotation axis must lie close to the plane of its orbit.

The density of Pluto is similar to that of water and it may be mainly a snowball of frozen methane with only a small rocky core.

Pluto is unusual among the planets because its orbit is very elliptical and inclined at the comparatively large angle of 17° to the **ecliptic**. In fact, Pluto spends a proportion of its orbital period of 248 years lying closer to the Sun than Neptune. This situation pertains from 1979 to 1999. Pluto's unusual orbit may be a clue to its origin. Pluto may once have been a satellite of

Neptune. Some disturbance may have ejected Pluto into its present independent orbit, Charon may have been torn out of Pluto, and Neptune's remaining satellite system left disrupted, as it appears today. Pluto was discovered in 1930 after extensive searches. Perturbations in the expected motions of Uranus and Neptune led astronomers to predict that the gravitational influence of an unknown ninth planet was responsible. Actually Pluto is far too small to be such an influence, and good fortune largely contributed to its discovery. There may yet be a tenth planet which approached Neptune long ago and exerted gravitational pull strong enough to cause havoc to Neptune's moons.

See also: Solar System for table of planetary data.

Pole Star or Polaris

The brightest star in the constellation Ursa Minor (Little Bear) which currently happens to lie within a degree of the North celestial Pole.

See also: precession, Plough, celestial sphere.

Praesepe

An open **star cluster** in the constellation Cancer, popularly known as the Beehive. Its presence is just about apparent to the naked eye, though a small telescope or binoculars are needed to reveal individual stars.

Precession

The slow change in direction of the Earth's rotation axis.

Over a period of 25,800 years, the Earth's axis sweeps out a cone in space of angular radius 23½° around the perpendicular to the plane of the Earth's orbit. The chief physical origin of this effect is the gravitational pull of the Sun and Moon on the Earth's equatorial bulge, the Earth's shape not being a perfect sphere. The complex motion of the Moon over a 19-year period causes a "wobble" on the smooth progress of precession, about 9 arc seconds in size. This effect is called nutation.

Precession has a number of consequences. One of these is that, after nearly 13 thousand years, the North celestial Pole will have traced out a semicircle in the sky. The nearest bright star to the pole will be Vega.

Since astronomers measure the coordinates of celestial objects in a system based on the point where the equator crosses the **ecliptic**, precession is constantly changing the **right ascension** and **declination** of all objects. Positional accuracy is now so great that precession has to be taken into account to the nearest year. This effect is called the precession of the equinoxes, because the points where the ecliptic and equator cross, also known as the equinoxes, seem to move slowly westwards around the ecliptic, taking 25,800 years to complete a whole circuit.

Prime focus see telescope

Prominence

Streamers of glowing gas visible in the outer layers of the **Sun**.

Astronomers recognise several types of solar prominences. Basically all are plumes of gas in the upper **chromosphere** and lower **corona**. They are visible because they have a higher density and lower temperature than the surrounding gas, which is transparent. Photographs and films give the superficial impression that prominences are tongues of fire leaping into the corona, but in fact they are relatively cool and dense. Although they are best seen when they extend beyond the solar disc, they are also detectable above the **photosphere**.

Among the various types of prominences are the rare and energetic eruptive prominences, which are spectacular surges associated with solar active regions. Loop prominences are tubes of gas flowing along magnetic field loops. Quiescent prominences last the longest, surviving several solar rotations. They arise as cool material cascades from the corona back to the photosphere.

Proper motion

The observed motion of a star across the **celestial sphere**, which is thus in a direction perpendicular to the observer's line of sight.

Proper motion results from the actual motion in space of a star relative to the Solar System. It is usually measured in seconds of arc per year. The more distant a star, the smaller its proper motion, even though its true space motion may be large. So, proper motions are only measurable for nearer stars. The star with the largest known proper motion is **Barnard's star**, a ninth magnitude red star, which is also the third nearest. It travels 10.3 seconds of arc each year.

Proxima Centauri

The nearest star to the Solar System.

Proxima Centauri is a small dim red star of **spectral type** M. Its name derives from its location in space. It is the nearest star to the Solar System (**parallax** 0.763 arc sec), and is seen in the constellation Centaurus, so it is invisible from northern latitudes. It belongs to the triple system of alpha Centauri. The other two members, α Centauri A and B, are much brighter than Proxima, so the whole system appears as the brightest star in Centaurus.

Proxima is a flare star. It suffers occasional outbursts when it brightens by up to four **magnitudes** for only a matter of minutes. These **flares** are similar in nature to those which occur on the Sun, but cause a relatively more dramatic effect in a star which is intrinsically so much fainter.

Ptolemy

An astronomer who lived between about A.D. 100 and A.D. 170 and worked in the city of Alexandria. His detailed, Earth-centred model of the Solar System was used until the **Copernican**, Sun-centred model took precedence in the 16th century.

According to the Ptolemaic system, the Sun, Moon and planets were carried around the Earth on moving spheres. In order to account for the known, uneven motion of these bodies, he refined a complicated scheme of **epicycles**, small circular movements, superimposed on the main orbit, or **deferent**. Furthermore, he supposed that the planets rotated uniformly, not about the Earth itself, but about a point in space, some distance from the centre, known as the equant.

These elaborate schemes were able to predict the positions of the planets and the Sun and Moon satisfactorily, taking into account the low degree of precision with which positions could be measured. Ptolemy was not concerned with a unified physical system which would account for all observations within a simpler framework. His scientific work was contained in a book which has become known as the Almagest. Claudius Ptolemy, the astronomer, should not be confused with the quite different Kings of Egypt of the same name.

Pulsar

A radio source, characterised by the rapidity and regularity of the bursts of radio waves it sends out.

Pulsars were discovered in 1967 by radio astronomers in Cambridge, England. The radio signals emitted by pulsars consist of a continuous series of sharp "bleeps" or regular pulses. The frequency of the pulses is remarkably regular. The time between successive pulses (the period) varies from one pulsar to another, and is between a quarter of a second and four seconds. Several hundred are already known, all within our own **Galaxy**, but probably many more remain to be discovered. The pulses occur because a pulsar is a rapidly-rotating star which emits a beam of radiation. One pulse is detected each time the beam sweeps past the Earth, rather like the way a lighthouse works.

Probably the most interesting and well-known pulsar is that which lies in the centre of the **Crab Nebula**. It is the only pulsar that astronomers can see flashing in visible light. X-ray and gamma-ray pulses from it have been detected too. The Crab Nebula pulsar holds the record for the shortest known period, only 0.033 seconds.

Pulsars have been identified with **neutron stars**, the immensely condensed remnants of exploded stars.

Q

Q.S.O.

Abbreviation for quasi-stellar object, or **quasar**.

Quadrant

An instrument formerly used by astronomers and navigators for measuring the **altitudes** of astronomical objects.

A quadrant consists of a quarter of a circle graduated in degrees, with a means of sighting a star, so that its altitude can be read from the scale. The accuracy of the instrument can be improved by constructing it on a large scale. Large mural quadrants were made. These had to be fixed to a wall in a permament position, and so they were usually placed in such a way that stars were observed as they crossed the **meridian**. One of the greatest exponents of the use of the quadrant was probably **Tycho Brahe** 1546–1601) who was renowned for his measurements of the positions of stars and planets.

The Mural Quadrant was at one time the name of a constellation, but is no longer used. However, the name is still attached to a meteor shower, the Quadrantids, whose radiant lies where the Quadrant used to be, now part of Boötes.

Quadrature

An alignment of the Moon or a planet, relative to the Earth and Sun, such that the angle between the lines joining the Sun to Earth, and Earth to the Moon of planet is 90°.

At quadrature, the **elongation** of a body is 90°.

See also: elongation and Fig. 10, page 44.

Quasar

A distant, compact, object beyond our **Galaxy** that looks starlike on a photograph but has a **redshift** characteristic of a very remote object.

The word "quasar" is a contraction of quasi-stellar object. In 1963 they were discovered as the optical counterparts of strong extragalactic **radio sources**. What distinguishes quasars is their high redshifts: many have a redshift of around 2, corresponding to a velocity four-fifths that of light, some nearly 4, which indicates a recession speed around nine-tenths the velocity of light. If these speeds are interpreted as the expansion of the universe the distances derived from the **Hubble Law** run into billions of **light years**. Although quasar redshifts have been the subject of acrimonious debate among astronomers, the balance of evidence currently favours the conventional application of the Hubble Law. Of course the fact that quasars are visible over such huge distances implies that they must be extraordinarily bright – up to a million times more luminous than giant **galaxies**. Since they are also variable, astrophysicists have deduced that most of this energy emerges from a region less than a light year in diameter. It is the unique combination of small size and high luminosity that sets a severe problem for theorists attempting to explain the energy source in quasars. It certainly cannot be the nuclear energy conventionally released in stars. One process that is sufficiently efficient is the energy release which takes place as matter rains down onto a supermassive **black hole**.

See also: blazar, radio astronomy.

R

Radar astronomy

The use of radar pulses to determine the distances, movements and structure of objects in the Solar System.

The radar technique consists of bouncing a pulse of high frequency radio waves from the object under study. The faint reflection can be detected by a radio telescope. Careful measurement of the time taken by the pulse to travel to the body and back gives an accurate means of measuring its distance because radio waves travel at the speed of light, which is known with great precision. This method has been used to obtain the value of the **Astronomical Unit** and hence the distance scale of the whole Solar System.

If the planet reflecting the radio waves is moving or rotating, the return pulse will suffer a **Doppler** shift. The varying size of the Doppler shift from different parts of the planet reveals the rotation speed. It was by this means that the true rotation period of Mercury first became known in 1965. Radar can also be used for mapping surface relief, and has been particularly useful in the case of Venus, whose surface is invisible because of the thick overlying layers of opaque cloud.

Radar astronomy is a technique which uses radio waves sent out from Earth to probe bodies in the Solar System. It is not concerned with radiations originating within these bodies.

Radio astronomy

The exploration of the universe by detecting the radio waves emitted by a variety of astronomical objects.

Radio astronomy started in the late 1940s essentially as a logical development of wartime radio science. In radio astronomy the natural radio emissions from cosmic objects are collected and analysed. Several types of radio telescope are in common use. The single dish antenna is similar to a **Newtonian** or **Cassegrain** reflecting telescope. Huge dishes, up to 100 metres across, are used in order to get a strong signal. Compared to light, radio waves are about a million times longer in wavelength, so the surface of a radio dish need not be as accurately figured as in an optical telescope. The long wavelength of radio waves means that a single-dish telescope has poor **resolving power**. By linking separate dishes it is possible to simulate a much larger dish; this technique is known as radio interferometry. Resolving powers down to a thousandth of a second of arc are possible by linking telescopes on different continents in what is known as very long baseline interferometry (VLBI). Such a link-up can pinpoint emission regions the size of our Solar System in **quasars** billions of **light years** away. There are even some "telescopes" that are nothing more than a bewildering array of wires and antennas that are "steered" across the sky by connecting different elements in a variety of ways. Such a telescope found the first **pulsars**.

The radio astronomer measures the intensity of radio emission at different points in the sky. This information can be listed in catalogues of radio sources, the most famous example of which is the Third Cambridge Survey or 3C catalogue. For an extended object a map showing the distribution of radiation may be made, and this can also be displayed rather like a photograph. Both continuum radiation, without obvious spectral lines, and line radiation at discrete wavelengths are detected. Sources of continuum radiation include radio galaxies, quasars, and hot gas nebulae. Line radiation comes from atoms, especially atomic hydrogen in the **Galaxy** at 21 cm, and also molecules; radio astronomy is a valuable technique for exploring the **interstellar medium**.

Radio astronomy spans a vast frequency range from about 10 megahertz to about 300 gigahertz (300 thousand million hertz). The equivalent wavelength range is from 30 metres down to 1 millimetre. Spectroscopy takes two forms: tuning a receiver across a narrow frequency range, as is done for spectral line radiation when it is desirable to measure the frequency of a line with great precision; and measuring the signal strength of several widely-spaced points across the **spectrum**, using several telescopes or detectors at different frequencies, as is done for plotting a continuum spectrum.

Among the great discoveries largely made by radio

astronomers may be included **radio galaxies**, quasars, pulsars, and **inter-stellar** atoms and molecules.

Radio galaxy

About one **galaxy** in a million is an intense source of cosmic radio waves, and is known as a radio galaxy.

The radio power from a radio galaxy may be as high as 10^{38} watts, which is about a million times higher than the weak radio emission from normal galaxies. Furthermore, in normal galaxies the radio emission generally comes from hydrogen in the disc, whereas in radio galaxies it is typically from two radio clouds symmetrically disposed on each side of the galaxy. The separation of the radio lobes is from tens of thousands of **light years** up to a few million light years. The radio emission is synchrotron radiation, generated by electrons moving close to the speed of light through magnetic fields.

For thirty years the outstanding problem in extragalactic radio astronomy has been the explanation of the huge energy reserves needed to power the brightest radio galaxies. Nuclear reactions which power the stars are totally incapable of satisfying the energy demands. It seems likely that gravitational energy, perhaps released as matter, falling into very massive **black holes**, may be the answer. Since radio galaxies are so bright in radio telescope they can be detected at great distances – thousands of millions of light years – and they are therefore important to observational **cosmology** because they tell us about the properties of the **universe** at large distances.

Radio source see radio astronomy

Ranger Program

A series of nine spacecraft, launched by the United States between 1961 and 1965 to photograph the Moon from close quarters. Many thousands of photographs were returned.

Red giant

A name applied to members of a group of cool, red stars, typically between ten and a hundred times larger than the Sun, and several hundred times more luminous.

Red giants are stars in an advanced stage of evolution. Internal changes, associated with the exhaustion of hydrogen by nuclear reactions in the central core, result in the expansion of the outer layers. Although the surface temperature drops too, the great increase in size produces a net gain in luminosity. The term "giant" is used to contrast with "**dwarfs**" of the same temperature. The giants occupy an area in the upper right part of a **Hertzsprung-Russell diagram**. The dwarf stars constitute the Main Sequence which runs in a band from the upper left to lower right. Two well-known red giant stars are Aldebaran in Taurus and Arcturus in Boötes.

See also: stellar evolution, star.

Redshift

The displacement of features in the **spectra** of astronomical objects, particularly **galaxies** and **quasars**, towards longer wavelengths, generally interpreted as a result of their recessional motion, the observable result of the **Doppler effect**.

"Redshift" has entered the astronomical language because the general expansion of the Universe means that all but the nearest of galaxies, whose local motions predominate, are receding from us. The opposite effect, blueshift, is thus much less commonly encountered in galaxies. Redshift is quantified as the ratio of the wavelength increase to the wavelength which would be observed if the object were at rest. The simple relation between their redshift and distance for galaxies is known as **Hubble's Law**.

A redshift may be produced in the presence of a strong gravitational field, according to the General Theory of **Relativity**, but the redshifts of galaxies are usually interpreted as being due to the Doppler effect alone, as it is believed that the gravitational contribution is very small in comparison. The gravitational redshift of light leaving the surface of the Sun is, however, measurable.

For a quarter of a century or more there has been increasing debate as to whether the observed redshifts of galaxies are truly due to recession in an **expanding universe**. The largest redshifts indicate objects moving away at 90 per cent of the velocity of light. The expanding universe hypothesis has the strongest support but is nevertheless questioned by some astronomers.

Reflector see telescope

Refractor see telescope

Relativity

The theory developed by Einstein which showed that concepts such as absolute space and absolute velocity are invalid in physics. All measurements of physical quantities have to be considered relative to the observer.

The special theory, published in 1905, arose from work on the laws of electromagnetism and dynamics. An important aspect of the theory is that the speed of light is the same for all observers and in all directions and is independent of the speed of the source. Another principle is that space and time are not to be considered as separate; they are not independent of each other and must be regarded as components of four-dimensional **spacetime**. The special theory shows how the laws of physics can be recast into an invariant form that is the same for all observers. Actual physical quantities such as mass, velocity and length are not, however, invariant; their magnitude depends on the relative velocity of the object and the observer.

At low speeds (everyday life) there is no significant difference between the laws of dynamics in classical and relativistic physics. At high velocities, approaching the speed of light, the differences are very marked.

In 1916 Einstein published the general theory of relativity, a landmark in the history of theoretical physics. In this he sought to unify spacetime and gravitation. The essential feature of this theory is that the presence of matter causes curvature, or bending, in the local spacetime grid. This curvature in turn controls the motion of other matter and is experienced as a gravitational force. Einstein thus accounted for **gravity** as an aspect of the curvature of spacetime.

Since the universe at large may be considered as a collection of big masses (galaxies) in a huge volume of spacetime, the general theory of relativity is of paramount importance in **cosmology**. This theory dominates the properties of the **universe** on the grandest scales, and it determines the overall structure and appearance of the universe. Within the framework of general relativity a rich variety of model universes may be derived mathematically. It is only by observation that we can determine which of these mathematical possibilities comes closest to reality.

From time to time it is claimed that the general theory has been overthrown or replaced. It is true that other theories have been advanced. However, Einstein's theory has withstood successfully every test that has ever been made of it and no observation that is definitely at odds with the theory has ever been made. The most famous test, perhaps, was made at the 1919 eclipse. Astronomers found that the bending of a ray of starlight that passed close to the Sun was precisely in accordance with the theory.

See also: black hole.

Resolving power

The ability of a **telescope**, or other optical instrument, to distinguish, as separate objects, two images which are close together.

Theoretically, the resolving power of a telescope is limited by the diameter or aperture of the primary mirror or **objective** lens. The larger the diameter, the better the telescope's performance. The limiting factor is the phenomenon of the diffraction of light, the bending of the paths of light rays when they encounter an obstacle. Because of diffraction, the images of stars are not true points, but small discs whose extents depend on the aperture of the telescope. The larger the aperture, the smaller the apparent image size and the easier it is to distinguish close objects. In practice, earth-bound telescopes are usually limited in performance by unsteadiness in the Earth's atmosphere which causes the images to dance about. This effect of the atmosphere is described as the quality of "**seeing**". The Space Telescope, which is expected to be launched above the atmosphere in the mid-1980s, will be the first professional optical telescope to operate at the diffraction limit. With its great resolving power astronomers expect to be able to distinguish very close pairs of stars, for example.

See also: radio astronomy.

Retrograde motion

The apparent change in direction of the path of a planet through the sky in which it is seen to be moving from east to west, in contrast to the normal sense of west to east. Also, any orbital or rotational motion opposite in direction to that considered normal.

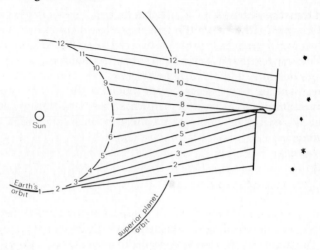

Fig. 23. The apparent retrograde motion of a superior planet is the result of the Earth "overtaking" the slower moving, more distant planet.

The retrograde motion of a planet arises from its orbital motion relative to the Earth's, when it is close to **opposition**, and the Earth "overtakes" it. The retrograde motion is temporary, and the net result is that the planet's path against the background of stars contains a loop. A satellite or moon which is orbiting its parent body in the sense that is opposite to that body's own rotation is said to have a retrograde orbit. Similarly, comets orbiting the Sun in the sense opposite to that of the major planets are said to have retrograde orbits.

Right ascension

One of the coordinates, used with **declination**, for specifying the positions of objects on the **celestial sphere**.

Right ascension (R.A.) is the celestial equivalent of longitude on the Earth. Circles of right ascension all intersect at the North and South celestial Poles, and cross the equator and other circles of declination at right angles. Right ascension is measured in hours, rather than degrees. The sphere of the sky is divided into twenty-four 15° segments. Each of these segments is one hour of right ascension, and each is further divided into minutes and seconds of time; so one minute of right ascension is equivalent to an angle of 0°.25. The use of hours to measure right ascension arises from the fact that the Earth's daily rotation causes the celestial sphere to appear to move through 1 hour of R.A. in 1 hour of **sidereal time**.

The zero of right ascension is set at one of the two points where the equator and **ecliptic** intersect, namely the position of the Sun on the vernal **equinox**. This point is variously termed the "**First Point of Aries**" and the "vernal equinox". The effects of **precession** cause this point to move very slowly along the equator, a difficulty which means that very accurate positions given in right ascension and declination have to include a correction for the time of observation.

See Fig. 2 on page 18 and Fig. 8 on page 42.

S

Saros

The period of about 18 years, after which a series of lunar and solar **eclipses** is repeated in approximately the same sequence.

The occurrence of eclipses depends on the exact alignment of the Sun, Moon and Earth. The complex motion of the Moon in orbit about the Earth repeats itself over a cycle of 6,585.32 days, or about 18 years, so each saros brings a similar sequence of eclipse events.

Satellite

Any body, whether natural or man-made, in a closed orbit around a larger body, its primary, whose gravitational attraction prevents the satellite from escaping.

Thousands of artificial satellites have been placed in orbit around the Earth since the first, Sputnik 1, launched by the Soviet Union in 1957. These are used for surveillance, telecommunications, weather forecasting, etc. The Earth's only natural satellite is the Moon, and the term "moon" is often used to describe the natural satellites of other planets.

Saturn

The sixth major planet of the **Solar System** in order from the Sun, and the second largest, which is surrounded by an extensive and famous ring system.

Saturn is a giant planet, second in size only to Jupiter. It has the lowest density of all the planets, only 0.7 times the density of water. This means that a typical piece of Saturnian matter would float in water. The low density arises because Saturn is predominantly gaseous, probably consisting mainly of hydrogen and helium. Features due to methane and ethane are also present in Saturn's spectrum. The visible disc of Saturn is actually the top of layers of cloud in the upper atmosphere. There are belts running parallel to the equator, but these are less prominent than the similar features on Jupiter. Very occasionally white spots appear on Saturn and last for some days or weeks, but spots on Saturn are not nearly so common nor so prominent as those on Jupiter. The period of rotation varies between 10 hours at the equator and 11 hours at the poles as the material is not solid. The rapid rotation makes Saturn the most oblate of all the planets, the polar radius being 11 per cent smaller than the equatorial radius.

To the telescopic observer, Saturn's rings are the most obvious feature, even in a small instrument, except for the occasions when the rings are apparently edge-on. As the rings are only a few kilometres thick, they essentially disappear from view when they are edge-on. This happens about every fifteen years. The rings are tilted at nearly 27° to the plane of Saturn's orbit, so the relative motion of the Earth and Saturn changes the angle at which the rings appear. The rings actually consist of large numbers of individual particles, each a tiny satellite of Saturn. The particles are thought to be several centimetres in size.

There are four distinct rings, known as rings A, B, C and D working from the outside inwards. Rings A and B are the brightest and are separated by a gap, 2,600 km wide, known as the Cassini Division. Ring C lies immediately inside Ring B, but is fainter. It is sometimes called the Crepe Ring. Ring D is even more tenuous, extending virtually into Saturn's atmosphere, and is separated from Ring C by a gap. The gaps are thought to be caused by the gravitational influences of Saturn's natural satellites. It is not known whether the rings condensed as they are when the Solar System formed, or whether they result from the break-up of a larger body.

DIMENSIONS OF SATURN'S RINGS

	Distance from in kilometres	Centre of Saturn in Saturn's radii (equatorial)
outer edge Ring D	72,600	1.21
inner edge Ring C	74,700	1.25
inner edge Ring B	90,600	1.51
outer edge Ring B	117,100	1.95
inner edge Ring A	119,800	2.00
outer edge Ring A	136,150	2.27

In addition to the ring system, Saturn has ten satellites. The largest, Titan, is known to be the largest satellite in the Solar System, and has an atmosphere containing methane and probably other gases. The sizes of Saturn's satellites are still rather uncertain.

SATELLITES OF SATURN

Number	Name	Probable Diameter (km)	Mean Distance from Saturn (km)	Orbital Period (days)
X	Janus	200	159,000	0.75
I	Mimas	500	186,000	0.94
II	Enceladus	600	238,000	1.37
III	Tethys	1,040	295,000	1.89
IV	Dione	820	377,000	2.74
V	Rhea	1,580	527,000	4.52
VI	Titan	5,830	1,222,000	15.95
VII	Hyperion	500	1,483,000	21.28
VIII	Iapetus	1,600	3,360,000	79.33
IX	Phoebe	200	12,950,000	550

See also: Solar System for table of planetary data.

Schmidt telescope

A reflecting **telescope** which uses a thin glass corrector plate to give high quality images over a wide field of view, which may be 10° or more in diameter.

This type of telescope was invented in 1930 by Bernhard Schmidt. Schmidt telescopes are particularly useful for photographing large areas of sky, and such telescopes built expressly for photographic work are often called Schmidt cameras. The photographic plate is fitted to the curved focal plane in a special holder. Large Schmidt cameras, such as the United Kingdom Schmidt telescope in Australia and the 1.2 m of the Hale Observatories at Palomar in California, have enabled extensive photographic surveys of the whole sky to be carried out.

The design principle of the Schmidt telescope may also be used to produce a compact, light-weight telescope for direct optical use. In practice, the **Cassegrain** system is often employed: a small secondary mirror is fitted behind the corrector plate, and the primary mirror has a central hole through which the light exits to an eyepiece or camera.

The primary mirror is figured as part of a sphere, rather than as a paraboloid, which is the usual shape for a conventional reflecting telescope. The glass corrector plate is thin, with a complex shape: it is thickest at the middle and around the edge. The shape can be calculated so that the plate exactly cancels the spherical aberration which would otherwise spoil the images at any distance from the optical axis of the telescope; the focal plane is, however, curved so the thin glass photographic plate has to be clamped in place.

The Schmidt telescope is the fundamental tool for astronomical survey work, when it is desirable to record all objects over a wide area of sky down to a faint **magnitude**. The plates taken with such telescopes have greatly increased the discoveries of faint asteroids and comets, and supernovae in distant galaxies. The deep survey plates have also enabled the radiations detected in **radio astronomy**, **X-ray astronomy** and **gamma ray astronomy** to be matched to optically-visible objects. For example, this was of importance historically for the discovery of **quasars**. The advent of very fast computers now enables photographic plates to be thoroughly analysed in a few hours. This development has increased still further the value of Schmidt telescopes, since such techniques demand the use of photographs of excellent quality.

Seeing

A term used by telescopic observers for the quality of observing conditions as influenced by the atmosphere.

In good seeing, images seen through the telescope appear steady and clear. In poor seeing conditions, images appear to shimmer, as if going in and out of focus. The image of a star, which ideally should be a tiny disc, may be a large, squirming circle of light. Thus, the performance of the telescope may be severely limited. The problem lies in turbulence in the Earth's atmosphere which bends the light rays away from their straight paths. The seeing is sometimes described by a scale from I to V, indicating extremely good or very poor. Typical average conditions would be termed III.

See also: resolving power.

Seyfert galaxy see galaxy

Shooting star see meteor

Sidereal

Pertaining to the stars, or heavenly bodies; or measured by reference to the stars, as in the case of sidereal time, sidereal month, etc. The word is derived from the Latin, "sidus", a star or astronomical body.

Sidereal month see month

Sidereal time see time

Skylab

A large space laboratory, launched unmanned into Earth orbit by the United States in 1973.

Between 1973 and 1974, three different three-man crews visited Skylab and worked there on biological, technical and astronomical experiments. This brilliant mission involved very careful liaison with scientists using ground-based telescopes. For nine months the Sun, particularly, was kept under surveillance by Skylab's battery of six telescopes, some of which could detect radiation that does not penetrate the Earth's atmosphere. Without doubt the Skylab results demonstrated the much greater flexibility that is possible if trained scientists can operate the equipment in space. The Skylab crews carried out important repairs to their space station. The scientific results greatly increased our knowledge of the Sun's atmosphere and outer layers.

Solar activity

A collective term for the many energetic phenomena which are observed to take place on the Sun.

Solar activity encompasses the occurrence of **sunspots**, solar **flares** and **prominences**. The level of activity on the Sun varies more or less regularly with an 11-year period. At the minimum level of activity, the Sun is said to be "quiet". Sunspots are rare and small. At maximum, the Sun's disc is never free of spots and flares occur more frequently.

Solar constant

A measure of the total amount of solar radiation received at a particular place, usually the Earth's surface if no location is quoted.

The solar constant is measured as the quantity of radiated energy passing perpendicularly through a unit of area at the top of the atmosphere in a given time. The value at the average distance of the Earth from the Sun is about 1.373 kilowatts per square metre. The measurements are today made from satellites or balloons. Some theoretical astrophysicists have speculated that the Sun's energy output varies, in which case the solar constant would change; for this reason the alternative expression "solar parameter" is now often used.

Solar System

The Sun and its retinue of **planets, satellites**, and related objects.

The Solar System comprises nine major planets and about 40 natural satellites, the minor planets (**asteroids**), **comets**, meteoroids, and the interplanetary medium. With the exception of the comets, the objects are confined to one plane, and the major planets all circle the Sun in the same sense. Almost all of them, and the Sun, rotate on their own axes in this same sense. The objects circling the Sun account for only 0.15 per cent of the mass of the Solar System but almost all (98 per cent) of its angular momentum. The common rotational properties must reflect the formation of the Solar System from a rotating gas cloud about five billion years ago. The total size of the Solar System is enormous – 100,000 astronomical units – if it is taken to include the orbits of the comets.

See also: accretion.

Planet	Mean distance from Sun (Astronomical Units)	Orbital Period	Equatorial diam (km)	Period of rotation on axis (relative to stars)	mass (Earth = 1)	volume (Earth = 1)	No of natural satellites
Mercury	0.39	87.97 days	4,880	58.65 days	0.06	0.06	0
Venus	0.72	224.70 days	12,104	243.0* days	0.82	0.86	0
Earth	1.00	365.26 days	12,756	23.93 hours	1.00	1.00	1
Mars	1.52	686.98 days	6,794	24.62 hours	0.11	0.15	2
Jupiter	5.20	11.86 years	142,800	9.84 hours	317.89	1323	14
Saturn	9.54	29.46 years	120,000	10.23 hours	95.17	752	10
Uranus	19.18	84.01 years	52,400	16–28 hours	14.56	64	5
Neptune	30.06	164.79 years	49,500	18–20 hours	17.24	54	2
Pluto	39†	247.7 years	3,000(?)	6.4 days	0.002	0.001	1

* Venus' rotation is retrograde – in the opposite sense to the orbital motion round the Sun.

† Pluto's very elliptical orbit causes its distance from the Sun to vary between 30 and 50 AU.

Solar wind

A moving stream of electrically-charged particles from the Sun, which has a velocity 400 kilometres per second at the Earth.

The solar wind is generated in the Sun's outer **corona**, particularly in the low density, cool regions known as coronal holes. Here the Sun's magnetic field lines splay out into space, and electrically-charged matter (protons, electrons) can flow away relatively freely. The wind may be picturesquely described as evaporation: the hot corona boiling off into interplanetary space. The solar wind deflects the tails of **comets** as they pass through the inner Solar System.

Solstices

The two occasions in the year when the Sun's position reaches its maximum distance from the celestial equator, or the actual positions of the Sun at these two times.

The solstices occur on about June 21 and December 21. These dates are commonly called midsummer's or midwinter's day (which is which depending on whether one is in the northern or southern hemisphere). On June 21, the Sun reaches declination $+23\frac{1}{2}°$, and is overhead at the Tropic of Cancer (latitude $23\frac{1}{2}°N$). On December 21, the Sun reaches declination $-23\frac{1}{2}°$ and is overhead at the Tropic of Capricorn (latitude $23\frac{1}{2}°S$).

Spacetime

We are familiar with the three dimensions of space. To these, physicists have added a fourth dimension, time. The unison of space-like and time-like dimensions makes a four-dimensional structure called spacetime.

Einstein's theory of **relativity** showed that location in space and time cannot be regarded as separate entities. Physical laws have to be considered against a background framework of both space and time. To specify the position of a particle, for example, we need three position coordinates and a time, giving four quantities in all. Abstractly we can imagine a "space" with four dimensions instead of three; this abstraction, in which the equations of physics take on an elegantly simple form, is termed spacetime.

On an ordinary map, two sets of coordinate lines, such as the lines of latitude and longitude, will allow us to specify uniquely the position of a point. The map can be envisaged as having a two-dimensional network or grid. Ordinary space clearly requires three dimensions, whereas spacetime has four dimensions. One of Einstein's important conclusions was that matter actually bends the four-dimensional grid of spacetime, or to put it simply: space is "curved" in the presence of matter.

For everyday purposes the three spatial dimensions suffice, since we all experience the same time coordinate: our clocks all run at the same rate and are synchronised by a worldwide system of radio signals. Over the immense distances encountered in astronomy the time factor for the travel of light signals becomes important. Also, at high relative velocities clocks no longer run at the same rates. In order to understand the geometrical properties of the universe it is, therefore, essential to deal with the four coordinates of spacetime.

Spectral line see spectrum

Spectral type

A classification assigned to a **star** on the basis of the appearance of its **spectrum**.

The system of classification of stellar spectra in use now divides stars among a number of main groups, designated by letters of the alphabet. The sequence of classes, in order of decreasing temperature is: O, B, A, F, G, K, M. This apparently random selection of letters has its origins in the first attempts at classification at the beginning of the 20th century, when the letters A, B, C etc. were used. Later, this system was shown to include errors and duplication. Some of the classes were abandoned and the rest re-ordered. The list is universally recalled with the aid of the mnemonic: O Be A Fine Girl, Kiss Me!

The chief attributes of the spectra of each class are as follows:

Class	Star colour	Typical Star Temperature	Spectral Features
O	blue-white	40,000 °K	few lines, mainly of highly ionised lighter elements.
B	blue-white	20,000	neutral helium, weak lines of hydrogen and singly ionised lighter elements.

Class	Star colour	Typical Star Temperature	Spectral Features
A	white	9,000	strong hydrogen lines, weak lines of heavier metals.
F	white to creamy	7,000	many lines of neutral and singly ionised metals, weak hydrogen lines.
G	yellow	5,500	neutral metal lines dominate, and there are some molecular bands.
K	orange	4,000	neutral metal and molecular bands very strong.
M	red	3,000	even more molecular bands than in class K. Titanium oxide bands particularly strong.

Most classes are additionally subdivided into ten sub-classes from 0 to 9, for more precise classification. There are also a number of other letters used for stars with unusual spectra. At the hot end, Wolf-Rayet stars, named after their discoverers and sometimes called W or WR stars, are believed to be among the hottest stars known at perhaps 50,000 °K. The main characteristics of their spectra are the presence of emission lines and the near absence of absorption lines. Among the coolest stars, some whose spectra seem to show features of elements different from those in usual M stars are put in classes S, R or N. S stars contain the oxides of the heavier metals zirconium, yttrium and barium. R and N stars together form the group of carbon, or C stars, which appear to contain unusually large amounts of carbon. There are various other categories for stars of unusual composition whose spectra do not slot neatly into the main classification system.

In addition to the main classification which is basically according to temperature, but with some allowance for variance in composition, there is also a classification according to luminosity. Stars of the same temperature may differ greatly in intrinsic luminosity. This difference is reflected in minor differences in the spectra. Luminosity classes are designated by Roman numerals as follows:

luminosity class	star type	absolute magnitude of F star
I	supergiants	−7 to −5
II ⎫ III ⎭	giants	−3 0
IV	subgiants	+2
V	main sequence (dwarfs)	+3
VI	subdwarfs	+4
VII	white dwarfs	+12

THE SPECTRAL TYPES OF SOME BRIGHT STARS

Name	Temperature class	Luminosity class
Aldebaran	K5	III
Altair	A7	V
Betelgeuse	M2	I
Canopus	F0	I
Procyon	F5	IV
Rigel	B8	I
Sirius	A1	V
Sun	G5	V
Vega	A0	V

Spectrograph

An instrument for recording a **spectrum**.

Spectrographs are used in conjunction with optical telescopes to record spectra in the visible region of the electromagnetic spectrum and the near infrared and ultraviolet. The light collected by the telescope's objective mirror or lens is brought to a focus on the entrance slit. The beam is made parallel and then dispersion is achieved by means of a diffraction grating, which is essentially a mirror or glass plate engraved with numerous fine, parallel grooves. Much better dispersion is obtained with a grating than with a prism. The spectrum is recorded either photographically or by electronic imaging devices. The greater the dispersion that is produced (i.e. the distance over which the spectrum is spread), the greater the detail displayed in the spectrum. The dispersion is limited by the design and capability of the spectrograph, and by the faintness of the object under study. As fainter objects are considered, so it becomes more difficult to record a spectrum of higher dispersion.

Spectrographs are quite bulky pieces of equipment. Smaller ones are usually fitted at the **Cassegrain** focus. Really high dispersion work has to be done at telescopes with a coudé focus, which is completely fixed, and usually inside a room below the observatory floor, where the spectrograph is permanently housed.

Spectroscopic binary see binary star

Spectrum

The result of spreading a beam of radiation according to wavelength. If the radiation is white light, the spectrum is the familiar band of rainbow colours, but the term applies more generally to the effect of dispersing any type of radiation with wavelength.

Light is the narrow part of the complete electromagnetic spectrum to which our eyes are sensitive. Light behaves as a wave, and is physically a disturbance in linked electric and magnetic fields, hence the expression electromagnetic waves. Light waves of different wavelengths are recognisable to our eyes as light of different colours. The spectral colours red, orange, yellow, green, blue and violet are in order of decreasing wavelength. Outside the visible wavelength band there are electromagnetic radiations which can be detected by means other than seeing them. To the long wavelength side lie the infrared and radio. Wavelengths shorter than visible light belong to ultraviolet light, X-rays and gamma-rays.

A spectrum may be viewed directly if it is in the visible range, or it may be recorded by means of photography or electronically. The appearance of a spectrum, and the range of wavelengths covered depend on the nature of the source of radiation and the particular instrument used to detect it. Some astronomical objects emit radiation over practically the entire electromagnetic spectrum, or a large part of it, but only one section at a time can be recorded, as different wavelength regions require different techniques.

All objects with temperatures above absolute zero emit electromagnetic radiation simply by virtue of their warmth. This radiation forms a continuous spectrum: that is a smooth distribution of intensity with wavelength over some wavelength region. The hotter the object, the more radiation is emitted and the wavelength band covered reaches to shorter and shorter objects. For example, objects at room temperature emit infrared and radio waves. An ember in a fire emits light, too, which has a shorter wavelength than infrared radiation. Stars, as hot balls of gas, emit a continuous spectrum whose exact wavelength range depends on the temperature at the outer layers.

Radiation is also emitted, and absorbed by individual atoms and molecules, but only at certain precise wavelengths. Atoms of different elements and molecules of different compounds are each capable of absorbing or emitting radiative energy at a selection of particular wavelengths. The pattern of wavelengths is characteristic of each individual element or compound. A hot gas, such as the sodium in a street light or the neon in a shop sign, emits a number of sharply defined wavelengths which give the glowing gas its characteristic colour. In a **spectrograph** the spectrum of such a gas appears as a series of bright lines of different colours, and for this reason it is called an emission line spectrum. Each "line" is an image of the narrow slit used to select the light entering the spectrograph.

Gas atoms are also capable of absorbing radiation at the same wavelengths as they emit. A gas lying between an observer and a hotter source of a continuous spectrum produces an absorption line spectrum. The dark lines are also called Fraunhofer lines, particularly with reference to the solar spectrum.

The spectra of most **stars**, including the Sun, are absorption line spectra. The extent of the continuous spectrum and the lines which are present depend chiefly on the star's temperature. Some stars and **galaxies** and emission **nebulae** show emission lines in their spectra.

Speculum see telescope

Spiral galaxy see galaxy

Sputnik

The name given by the Soviet Union to the series of unmanned Earth satellites. The first of these, Sputnik 1, was launched in 1957 and became the first artificial satellite put into orbit round the Earth. It was followed by Sputniks 2 and 3 in 1957 and

1958. For a number of years, the word "Sputnik" was synonymous with "artificial satellite".

Star

A ball of matter, held together by **gravity**, and a source of radiation.

Our **Sun** is considered to be a typical star. The distinguishing feature of a star is the fact that it has (or has had) a vast internal energy source. A star is essentially hot and emits electromagnetic radiation of its own, some of which may be in the visible region of the spectrum. The properties of stars vary with their mass, age and chemical composition.

In the central core of a star, nuclear fusion reactions take place. This process supplies the star's power. The net effect of these reactions is the transmutation of hydrogen into helium, and other chemical elements. During the process, some mass is converted entirely into energy. Since stars are typically 70 per cent hydrogen, they have enormous reserves of fuel. About 28 per cent of the mass of a star is helium; 2 per cent accounts for all the other chemical elements. However these proportions do change as a star consumes its fuel. There are transformations in the nature and structure of a star as it progresses, inevitably, to eventual death. The ways in which stars change through their lifetimes are described as **stellar evolution.**

The minimum mass of material needed to make a star is about one-twentieth the mass of the Sun. Below this limit, the energy released as the matter falls together under its own gravity does not generate sufficient heat for nuclear reactions to get going. The most massive stars known would make about seventy Suns. A star's mass is one of the main factors governing its energy output. The more massive a star is, the greater its luminosity.

Even though stars are so massive, they remain gaseous because they are so hot. The hot gas tends to expand outwards, counteracting the gravity pulling the gas inwards. On balance, the two effects cancel. A star forms itself into a sphere whose temperature and density gradually decrease away from the centre. There is no firm "edge" to a star.

The **spectrum** of radiation a star produces is an important clue to its physical nature. Stars are often discussed and classified according to the appearance of their spectra. Each star is allotted to a **spectral type.**

During certain phases of its life, a star's energy output may fluctuate, either regularly or in an unpredictable way. Such stars are described as **variable**. Many stars are found in pairs, bound together by their mutual gravitational pull. They form **binary star** systems.

See also:Hertzsprung-Russell diagram.

Star cluster

A group of stars, physically associated in space. Clusters fall into three main categories: open clusters (also known as galactic clusters), globular clusters and stellar associations.

Open clusters may contain less than a hundred stars or up to several thousand. The stars are not packed together very closely, and may be so thinly spread that the cluster is barely recognisable as such. The dimensions of these clusters are typically a few **light years**. A number of open clusters are clearly visible to the naked eye. Among these are the **Pleiades** and the **Hyades**, both in the constellation Taurus, and **Praesepe** in Cancer. Many more can be seen with binoculars. Open clusters usually contain a number of hot, luminous stars which makes them easier to see. Open clusters are all located within the disc of the **Galaxy**, and so appear to lie within the **Milky Way**. This distribution contrasts sharply with that of the globular clusters.

Fig. 24. The open star cluster close to the star κ Crucis in the Southern Cross. (*Radcliffe Observatory photograph*)

Fig. 25. The globular star cluster Messier 13 in the constellation Hercules. *(Photograph from the Hale Observatories)*

Globular clusters are densely-packed balls of stars, typically containing between fifty thousand and a million separate stars within a diameter of 50 light years. Globular clusters are not confined to the galactic disc, but are distributed throughout the spherical **halo** surrounding the Galaxy, though they are concentrated towards the centre. They contain no hot, luminous stars. Their stellar content and distribution in space are evidence of their great age on the astronomical timescale; around ten thousand million years. This may be compared with some of the youngest open clusters such as the Pleiades which are only a few tens of million years old.

Another distinguishing feature of globular clusters is the chemical composition of their member stars. Compared with open cluster stars, or the Sun, these tend to be deficient in the elements heavier than helium. The number of known globular clusters in our Galaxy is of the order of one hundred. The brightest is Omega Centauri in the southern hemisphere.

The study of star clusters is important in astronomy since their members shared a common origin. Observations of the stars' properties now show how stars of different masses have developed at different rates during their lifetimes. The

Hertzsprung-Russell diagram for a cluster is an important tool in such studies.

Members of an open cluster are often identifiable by the motion in space which they have in common, but there are also obvious star groupings in which the stars are moving apart. These groups contain very young hot stars (usually of **spectral type** O and B) and are known as associations. It is assumed that the stars formed together and have been drifting apart ever since. Such associations of older stars are never seen, because the stars have separated into the general field of stars. The stars in the region of Orion's belt and sword are an example of an O–B association. The rotation of the Galaxy accelerates the disruption of loose open clusters and associations.

The use of large telescopes and electronic detectors has enabled the study of star clusters to be pursued effectively in galaxies beyond the Milky Way, where they are useful indicators of differences within and among galaxies.

Steady state theory

A model of the **universe** in which it is assumed that the average properties of the universe do not change with time.

In 1948 three British astronomers, Hermann Bondi, Tommy Gold and Fred Hoyle put forward a new cosmological model as an alternative to the **Big Bang** model. They assumed that the universe looks essentially the same at all times, extending from the infinite past and into the infinite future. Since the universe is in fact observed to be expanding, the steady state theory requires the continuous creation of new matter in order to conserve the average density while this expansion takes place. The required rate of creation is remarkably tiny: on average ten atoms per cubic kilometre per century. The philosophical attraction of this theory is that a steady state universe has no beginning, no end and no outer boundary.

The clash between this theory and the observations has been one of the great events in astronomy this century, a confrontation fought out at the limits of the observable universe. Essentially, observations of remote **galaxies** and **quasars** have tended to suggest that the universe is evolving rather than changeless. The distant parts do not have the same properties as does the local neighbourhood. Observations of the expansion suggest that its rate has varied with time, and that it is slowing down.

The strongest evidence against the steady state model comes from observations of the cosmic **microwave background radiation**, which suggest that the universe was hot and dense (the Big Bang) in the remote past.

At present the balance of evidence goes against the steady state model and continuous creation. Historically the theory can be seen as having been highly significant as a spur to rapid theoretical and observational developments between about 1955 and 1970, particularly in **radio astronomy** which provided the main tools for testing the theory.

See also: Cosmology.

Stellar evolution

The sequence of events and changes which happen to a **star** from its initial formation.

Expressions normally associated with the life cycle of a living creature have been freely borrowed by astronomers to describe the events which happen to stars. We talk of the birth, death and life-time of a star. However, the term evolution is also used to describe the sequence of events occurring in a single star. In the case of living things, evolution is a process which can only happen as generation succeeds generation.

It is believed that stars condense out of the **interstellar medium**. As material begins to collect together, a protostar is formed. Matter squashing together, pulled in by **gravity**, gets hot. When the temperature in the centre of a protostar becomes high enough, nuclear fusion reactions start spontaneously. Once under way, the nuclear processes release far greater quantities of energy. The necessary high temperature is maintained and radiation flows outward, making the star shine.

The basic fuel for these reactions is hydrogen, which constitutes about 70 per cent of a typical star's mass. As a result of the nuclear transformation, helium is made. Although the star begins with a huge supply of hydrogen, ultimately there will be none left in the central core where it is hot enough for reactions to take place. An adjustment has to occur. The core contracts and releases heat. This heat penetrates to the overlying layer of hydrogen until the temperature is high enough to start reactions in a shell of fresh fuel surrounding the old helium core. Simultaneously, the outer parts of the star expand, and the surface temperature drops. The core, gradually acquiring more helium, contracts until it is so hot that the helium starts to fuse into carbon. The star's diameter has now grown to be perhaps a hundred times larger than it was. Its colour becomes redder. It has become a **red giant**. After this, a whole sequence of inner contractions and different nuclear reactions can occur, but when all possible fuels are exhausted, the star shrinks and fades. **White dwarfs** are a class of faded and dim stars which have in this way reached the ends of their lives. However, stars whose masses exceed several times the Sun's seem to go out with a bang instead. **Supernovae** are the gigantic stellar explosions which signal the final stage of a more massive star. The dense core left after this cataclysmic event is a **neutron star.**

During certain stages of its later life, a star may become unstable, and pulsate either in a regular way, or irregularly. Variation in brightness accompanies the pulsation. The star becomes a **variable.**

The **Hertzsprung-Russell diagram**, which links luminosities with surface temperatures for a group of stars, is a particularly useful tool for astronomers studying stellar evolution. Such a diagram constructed for a **star cluster** shows how a sample of stars which are all of the same age, but cover a range of masses, has responded to the passage of time. It turns out that the rate at which a star progresses through the sequence of events depends on its starting mass. The more massive a star, the faster it dashes through its life-cycle. The main sequence in the Hertzsprung-Russell diagram is formed from points representing stars consuming hydrogen in the main phase of their life. Stars to the right of the main sequences are either still forming or are in more advanced stages of evolution. The oldest of all, the **white dwarfs**, lie in a group well below the Main Sequence. A combination of observational data and theoretical computational work has enabled astronomers to deduce the "tracks" which stars of different masses follow on a Hertzsprung-Russell diagram as they undergo changes in temperature and luminosity in the course of their evolution.

Subdwarf see dwarf

Sun

The central object of our Solar System and the nearest star to the Earth.

The Sun is at an average distance of almost 150 million

kilometres. On account of its proximity, it has been studied in far greater detail than any other star.

The source of solar energy, like that of stars generally, is the release of nuclear energy in the central core. Here the temperature is about 15 million degrees, and the density of matter is 155 times that of water. Under these circumstances the nuclei of hydrogen atoms collide hard enough to fuse into the second lightest element, helium. This nuclear reaction involves a slight mass loss (about half of one per cent), and this appears as pure energy, in the form of gamma rays. The high density and central temperature arise in the first place because the Sun is a very massive body, about one third of a million times more massive than the Earth. The crushing force of its own gravity compresses the material at the centre to the point where nuclear reactions occur spontaneously. The core extends to about one-quarter of the solar radius and it contains about one-half of all the mass. In terms of **stellar evolution**, our Sun is roughly half-way through its life-cycle, because the central nuclear furnace has consumed about half the hydrogen. At the centre some five million tons of matter are totally annihilated every second, releasing power at a rate of about 3×10^{23} kilowatts.

Away from the central core the temperature and pressure steadily decrease. Energy is carried some 85 per cent of the way to the surface as radiation. It then encounters the Sun's convection zone, a turbulent region where columns of hot gas race towards the surface. The surface layer, or **photosphere**, has a temperature of about 6,000 degrees. Above the photosphere are found, in successive order, the cool **chromosphere**, the inner **corona**, the outer corona, and finally the **solar wind** merging with interplanetary space.

The average density of the Sun is roughly 1.4 times that of water. Although the core is very dense, the average is pulled down by the extensive outer layers of gas. Like all large astronomical bodies the Sun rotates, around an axis that is tilted at 7° to the main plane of the Solar System. Unlike the Earth, the Sun does not rotate as a rigid body: the equatorial regions take about 25 days to complete one circuit and the poles take about 35 days. This differential rotation must cause stress in the internal magnetic field, as the equatorial region continuously laps the poles. Perhaps this is the underlying cause of the 11-year cycle of **solar activity**. Over most of the surface the magnetic field is not much stronger than the Earth's.

The Sun is located 10 **kiloparsecs** from the centre of the **Galaxy** and about 10 **parsecs** above the galactic plane. Its orbital speed in the Galaxy is 250 kilometres per second, which enables it to make one circuit every 220 million years. From a distance it is an average star: a **dwarf** of **spectral type** G2 V, and an absolute **magnitude** +4.8.

One of the current puzzles in astronomy is the solar **neutrino** flux. The neutrinos emerging from the Sun are rather scarcer than is indicated by the theory of stellar nuclear reactions, and the cause of the discrepancy is unknown.

Our Sun provides an essentially inexhaustible supply of energy. All forms of man-made energy (nuclear power, combustion of fossil fuels, hydroelectric power, tides, etc.) amount to only 0.01 per cent of the solar energy intercepted free-of-charge by the Earth. At present this solar energy makes only a tiny contribution to our energy consumption, but it is a contribution that must inevitably grow in importance.

For astronomers the Sun is of major consequence simply because it is so near. Solar astronomy probably accounts for one-fifth of all astronomical research activity. In the past the study of the Sun led to many important discoveries: the element helium, the source of stellar energy, and the solar wind, to name only three.

See also: aurora, chromosphere, corona, faculae, flare, Fraunhofer lines, granulation, magnetosphere, neutrino astronomy, nucleosynthesis, photosphere, prominence, solar activity, star, stellar evolution, sunspot, Van Allen belts.

Sunspot

An apparently dark area of the Sun's surface.

Regions of intense magnetism sometimes erupt into the solar **photosphere**, causing areas of intense activity. One aspect of this is the appearance of sunspots. Their dark interiors are dark only in contrast to the brilliant photosphere. The central portion of a sunspot (the Umbra) has a temperature of 4,000 °K, and its lighter periphery (the penumbra) about 5,500 °K. The magnetism is intense, being of the order of ten thousand times larger than the Earth's field, and it is the presence in the photosphere of the concentration of magnetism that causes the spot. Sunspot sizes cover a great range, from tiny pores to complex groups stretching a quarter of the way across the visible disc. Mostly they persist for a couple of weeks, although a big clump might last for two months.

Sunspots generally occur in pairs and complex groups. In a pair each spot has opposite magnetic polarity, as if a magnetic tube is leaving the surface at one spot, arching over, and re-entering at another.

It has been known for over a century that the average number of spots rises and falls semi-regularly on a cycle that takes about 11 years. At the start of a cycle spots are sparse and they occur at latitudes 30° from the equator. New spots grow progressively more numerous and closer to the equator. At the peak of the cycle they are clustered at latitudes 5°–10° from the equator. The cause of this cyclic behaviour must be a reaction of the internal magnetism to differential rotation.

Sunspots are only one aspect of energetic outbursts on the Sun. Other aspects include **faculae, flares** and **prominences**.

See also: butterfly diagram.

Supergiant

One of a small number of massive stars which are the largest and most luminous stars known.

The masses of supergiants range between 10 and 60 times the Sun's mass. They have several hundred times the Sun's diameter, and are more luminous by a factor 10,000 or more. Although supergiants are not common among stars, their enormous luminosity makes them visible at great distances, and many of the brightest stars in our sky are supergiants. They include Polaris, Betelgeuse, Deneb and Canopus.

See also: Hertzsprung-Russell diagram.

Superior conjunction see conjunction.

Superior planets

Those major planets in the Solar System whose orbits lie further from the Sun than the Earth's; namely: Mars, Jupiter, Saturn, Uranus, Neptune and Pluto.

Supernova

Rare and spectacular stellar explosion resulting in the destruction of a massive star.

The supernova explosion is one of the endpoints of **stellar evolution**, reserved for stars several times the mass of the Sun. Towards the end of its life a star has meagre energy supplies and it must adjust its structure if it is to continue to oppose the inward force of its own gravity. Supernova explosions arise in stars where the adjustment takes place catastrophically. The precise nature of the trigger for the explosion is not known, but basically what happens is that the central core (the exhausted nuclear reactor) collapses down, in less than one second, to a size of a few kilometres and the outer envelope of the star explodes. The central relic is probably a compact **neutron star** or **pulsar**, or perhaps even a **black hole** in extreme cases. The initial explosion velocity of the outer envelope may be one tenth the speed of light. It becomes transparent to light, and so can be seen shining brightly, when it has expanded to a sphere about 10^9 km in diameter. The expelled material eventually forms a supernova remnant.

At maximum brilliance a supernova reaches an **absolute magnitude** of about -15 to -20 which is at least 100 million times the Sun's magnitude and around 100 times brighter than an ordinary **nova**. The occurrence of a supernova cannot be predicted in advance. Since the astronomical use of the telescope none has been visually observed in our **Galaxy**. Supernovae in other galaxies are spotted as a result of regular patrol searches, usually made with **Schmidt telescopes**. The frequency of outbursts elsewhere suggests that, on average, three explosions per century take place in our Galaxy. Any that have occurred in the last 350 years have been obscured by the **interstellar medium**.

In the past bright supernovae are known to have been seen in A.D. 1006, 1054 (**Crab Nebula**), 1572 (**Tycho Brahe**'s supernova) and 1604 (**Kepler**'s supernova).

The expanding shells of supernovae become supernova remnants. These are detectable as sources of radio and X-ray emission. Eventually, after thousands of years, the beautiful tracery of the optical remnant is a conspicuous feature. The finest remnants include the Crab Nebula, the Vela remnant, and the Cygnus Loop.

In the supernova outburst, elements in the outer envelope are processed by explosive nuclear reactions to form heavier elements. Explosive **nucleosynthesis** is an important mechanism for creating the heavier elements in the universe and distributing them through the Galaxy. A supernova remnant eventually merges with other interstellar clouds, enriching them with extra supplies of heavy elements. Over billions of years supernova explosions therefore increase the proportion of heavy elements in newly-formed stars.

Surveyor program

An American space program which soft-landed unmanned probes on the Moon between 1966 and 1968 as a preliminary to the manned **Apollo** landings.

Out of seven Surveyors launched, five were successful. They carried out experiments on the strength, composition and structure of the surface of the Moon, and proved that a manned landing would be possible. The Surveyors also returned thousands of pictures of the lunar panorama. Parts of Surveyor 3 were recovered and returned to Earth by the Apollo 15 mission.

Synodic month see month, phase

Synodic period

The average time taken by a planet to return to the same position in its orbit, relative to the Earth. In the case of the Moon, the synodic **month** is the interval between successive new Moons, 29.53059 days. For a planet, the synodic period could be determined as the average time interval between successive oppositions, for example.

Syzygy

A term applied to the situation when the Sun, Earth and Moon, or the Sun, Earth and another planet lie roughly in a line. The term Syzygy, therefore, describes both **conjunctions** and **oppositions**.

T

Tektite

Small glassy bead found on the Earth's surface, probably created as the result of meteoric impact.

Tektites are glassy objects, usually no more than a couple of centimetres in size, variously found in the shape of a button, sphere, pear, or lens. Their shapes indicate that they solidified from molten material that cooled rapidly as it travelled through the atmosphere. They are found strewn on the surface only in certain parts of the world: in Czechoslovakia and western Australia particularly, and as microtektites they occur in ocean sediments. Their ages range up to 30–40 million years. It is likely that the strewn fields resulted from major **meteorite** impacts that splashed molten rock across a wide area.

Telescope

An instrument designed to collect radiation (e.g. light, radio waves) from a distant object, bring the radiation to a focus and produce a magnified image or signal. Telescopes used by astronomers can be broadly classified as optical, radio, or X-ray telescopes, for example, according to the type of radiation detected.

Optical telescopes fall into two main categories: refractors and reflectors, according to whether the main light-gathering component, or objective, is a lens or a mirror. A refracting telescope has an **objective** lens at the front of the telescope tube, and either an eyepiece at the back, with which the image is viewed, or a camera or other equipment. In a reflecting telescope the objective is a concave mirror at the back of the tube. The light comes to a focus in front of the main mirror, at a position called the prime focus, from where it is usually redirected to a place where the image can be viewed more conveniently, by means of a small secondary mirror. There are a number of different

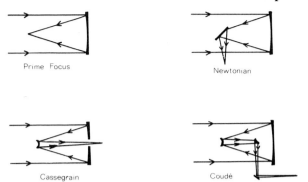

Fig. 26. Four different optical arrangements which are used in the construction of reflecting telescopes.

arrangements commonly used: the **Newtonian**, the **Cassegrain** and the **Coudé**. In very large telescopes the observer may be able to sit directly at the prime focus. The obstruction caused by secondary mirrors, or a prime focus cage, has little effect on the performance of the telescope in practice.

All large astronomical telescopes are reflectors because of the inherent difficulties in constructing and mounting glass lenses of large diameter. The world's largest refractor, completed in 1897, has an objective of 102 cm (40 inches) in diameter, and belongs to the Yerkes Observatory in Wisconsin, U.S.A.

The mirrors in reflecting telescopes are made from glass, which is carefully figured to the required shape, either part of a sphere or part of a paraboloid. A thin layer of aluminium is then deposited onto the glass to provide the reflecting surface. Early reflectors were made from speculum metal, and the abbreviation "spec" is still sometimes used for a mirror. The tube of a reflector is often just an open framework supporting the optical components.

The **Schmidt** and **Maksutov** telescopes are basically reflectors, but they employ a thin correcting lens at the front of the tube to provide good images over a wide field of view and yet be of a compact size.

The faintest objects which can be seen with a telescope depend on the size of the objective which governs the light-gathering power. The **resolving power** of a telescope also increases with the size of its aperture. The magnification which can be achieved is generally a secondary factor in astronomical use. Different magnifications are achieved by using different eyepieces. However, when viewing stars, the main effect is to change the size of the field of view, as the images of stars are always the same small discs of light, however great the magnification. For viewing objects with detectable structure, the greatest useful magnification is limited usually by the quality of seeing, though larger telescopes generally are able to tolerate larger magnifications. The images formed by astronomical telescopes are inverted (upside down) as there is no useful purpose served by introducing extra lenses to rectify the image. Such lenses would only reduce the total amount of light reaching the observer's eye.

The mounting of an astronomical telescope is an important part of its structure, since an observer needs to be able to point the instrument easily at selected objects, and follow them as the Earth's rotation causes the apparent movement of the sky. Small amateur telescopes and very large computer controlled telescopes may employ the **altazimuth** mount. Probably the most commonly used system is the **equatorial mount**.

Most astronomical telescopes have "finder" telescopes mounted on them. The finder is a small, low-power telescope with cross-wires marking the centre of the field of view. It is lined up so that objects on the cross-wire in the finder are in the field of view of the main telescope, which will be much smaller. This is an important aid to locating the objects the observer wishes to find. Another aid is setting circles on an equatorial mount. The observer simply turns the telescope in **right ascension** and **declination** until the scales on the setting circles read the coordinates of the object he is seeking.

For descriptions of radio telescopes and X-ray telescopes see radio astronomy and X-ray astronomy respectively.

Terminator

The boundary between the region on the surface of a planet or Moon which is illuminated by the Sun, and the part of the surface which is in shadow.

Tides

The distortion of a star or planet resulting from the differences between the gravitational forces acting on different parts of it.

The most familiar examples of tidal action are the tides produced in the oceans by the gravitational influence of the Moon. The Moon's pull causes two bulges in the oceans, one directed towards the Moon, and one on the opposite side of the Earth. The far bulge occurs because the gravitational force there is weaker than the average force acting on the solid sphere of the Earth. The size of tides is exaggerated when the Sun and Moon are in line, at new Moon and full Moon, so that the Sun reinforces the Moon's gravity. This situation produces spring tides. When the Sun is 90° away from the Moon its pull acts partly to counteract the lunar tide, and low neap tides occur. At any coastal place, the precise timing and the height of the tide will depend to a certain extent on the local conditions, though the position of the Moon is the primary influence. Generally, there are two high tides in every period of 24 hours 50 minutes.

Time

The means by which the order and separation of sequential events are described.

Accurate timekeeping is important both for civil purposes and scientific measurements. In the past, scientists have used various devices to keep track of time, continuing a search for more accurate and reliable methods. As the day and the year are the most important intervals of time where human affairs are concerned, the rotation period of the Earth on its axis and the orbital period of the Earth about the Sun are fundamental units of time. Since 1972, however, atomic clocks have been used as the main basis of timekeeping. The atomic vibration used as the measure of time in these clocks does not suffer from the small irregularities which affect the Earth's motion.

Civil time in most parts of the world is based on Universal Time, which is the mean solar time at the Greenwich meridian. Mean solar time follows the average, smoothed rate at which the Sun moves around the sky. The real Sun moves at a rate which is apparently variable because of the ellipticity of the Earth's orbit and the tilt of the Earth's axis. As a result, time measured by means of a sundial (local solar time) usually differs from the mean local time by an amount which may be as large as 16.4 minutes.

The mean local time at a place differs from Universal Time (U.T.) according to longitude. For every degree west, local time is 4 minutes later and for every degree east, 4 minutes earlier than the time on the Greenwich meridian. For convenience, most countries adopt one or more time zones throughout which the civil time is taken to be the same, regardless of actual local variation.

Universal Time, being based on the rotation of the Earth, suffers from small fluctuations compared with the ideal, smooth-flowing time assumed in calculating the future positions of the Sun, Moon and planets. For this reason, tables of planetary positions (ephemerides) were given in terms of a totally uniform Ephemeris Time (E.T.). In 1972 Ephemeris Time was replaced by International Atomic Time (T.A.I.).

The rotation of the Earth relative to the stars, rather than the Sun, forms the basis of sidereal time which is primarily of interest to astronomers. The sidereal day is 23 hours 56 minutes 4.091 seconds of solar time, and is the interval between successive passages of any particular star across the observer's meridian. The sidereal time at any instant is the right ascension of the meridian. Thus, the sidereal time tells astronomers which stars are visible. Observatories almost always have a clock showing sidereal time. In practice, Universal Time is followed by observations of the stars in terms of sidereal time. The relationship between U.T. and sidereal time is accurately known, so the conversion can be made.

Titius-Bode Law see Bode's Law

Transient lunar phenomenon (T.L.P.)

A small, temporary obscuration or glow on the otherwise unchanging surface of the Moon.

It is now generally accepted that T.L.P.s do occur from time to time, particularly in the border regions of mare basins. They are probably the result of the release of trapped gases, rather than any real volcanic activity.

Transit (1)

The passage of a star or other astronomical object across the observer's **meridian**. **Circumpolar stars** may be observed at both upper and lower transits.

Transit (2)

The passage of one astronomical body across the disc of another, as viewed from Earth. The term is applied particularly to the crossing of moons over the disc of their primary planets, and to the passage of the planets Mercury and Venus across the face of the Sun.

Typically, the inclinations of the planetary orbits cause Venus and Mercury to pass above or below the Sun at inferior conjunction. When the geometry is right, however, the small dark discs of these planets may be seen to cross the Sun. Transits of Mercury are the commoner. They take place in May or November at regular intervals which are either 7, 13 or 46 years for November transits, 13 or 46 years for May transits. Transits of Venus occur in pairs. The two transits in a pair are 8 years apart, but the gaps between successive pairs are over a hundred years.

Transits of Mercury

1960 November 7
1970 May 9
1973 November 10
1986 November 13
1993 November 6
1999 November 15

Transits of Venus

1639 December 4
1761 June 5
1769 June 3
1874 December 8
1882 December 6
2004 June 7
2012 June 5

Twilight

A period of time immediately following sunset or preceding sunrise when the sky is bright with sunlight scattered in the air.

Twilight is defined more precisely in terms of the Sun's distance below the horizon. Astronomical twilight is the period when the Sun is less than 18° below the horizon. During this time, the sky is too bright for many types of astronomical work.

The duration of twilight varies according to latitude and the time of the year. The times of twilight are given in astronomical tables along with sunrise and sunset.

For civil purposes, twilight is defined as the time when the Sun is less than 6° below the horizon. It is still nautical twilight when the Sun is between 6° and 12° below the horizon.

Tycho Brahe

A Danish astronomer who lived between 1546 and 1601, often known just as Tycho.

Tycho was the outstanding observational astronomer of his time. Though he worked before the telescope came to be used in astronomy, he made positional measurements on the stars and planets which were, for the time, unrivalled in accuracy. His observations provided the data for the work of his younger colleague **Kepler**, who derived from them the laws governing the orbits of the planets. Tycho himself maintained that the Earth lay at the centre of the Solar System, the Sun and Moon orbiting around it, but that the other five planets were in orbit around the Sun. This model never gained general acceptance. Tycho was fortunate enough to witness a bright **supernova** in 1572 which lay in the constellation Cassiopeia and reached an **apparent magnitude** of −4. This supernova is sometimes called Tycho's star.

U

UHURU

The first **X-ray astronomy** satellite launched from Kenya in 1970. It made the first good map of the X-ray sky and demonstrated the rich variety of phenomena detectable by X-ray telescopes.

Ultraviolet astronomy

Detection and analysis of radiation at wavelengths between 25 and 350 nanometres.

Ultraviolet astronomy spans the wavelength gap between optical and **X-ray astronomy**. It has to be carried out using high-altitude balloons, rockets or satellites, because almost all ultraviolet radiation is absorbed in the Earth's lower atmosphere. Important sources of ultraviolet radiation include the Sun and the hot blue-white stars. The hottest stars emit much of their radiation in the ultraviolet.

Unidentified Flying Object (U.F.O.)

A term loosely applied to any sighting in the sky which the observer is unable to account for in terms of known phenomena.

Most of the public interest in unidentified flying objects centres around the possibility that intelligent beings from space might be responsible for them. U.F.O. reports can be divided roughly into three categories:

(1) Hoaxes: None of the more extravagant claims concerning flying saucers and visitors from space have ever been substantiated by reputable investigators. Some hoaxers have been exposed or have confessed.

(2) Lack of knowledge on the part of the observer: Many of the apparently unusual things that appear in the sky do have perfectly ordinary explanations which may not be appreciated at

the time by oberservers who do not have the appropriate knowledge or experience. Meteors, bright planets, bright twinkling stars, aircraft lights, artificial satellites, weather balloons, reflections in car and aircraft windows are commonly confused. (3) Genuine unexplained phenomena: There undoubtedly remain a number of observations which have not been adequately explained. However, there seems no reason to resort to extraterrestrial intelligence as their origin at the moment, as nature still holds many secrets. They should be thoroughly investigated as they will probably lead to new scientific discoveries.

Universe

The totality of all that can affect us by means of physical forces.

The word universe does not, perhaps, have rigorous meaning. It has several synonyms: space, the heavens, the cosmos. The concept is influenced by Society and culture also, for our ideas about the scale of the universe are limited by the horizons of the available means of exploration and discovery. To the Greeks, for example, the word "universe" meant a very much smaller affair than we would consider today. Even into the early part of the twentieth century the distant galaxies were spoken of as if they were "other" universes.

In modern astronomy the term is normally used to encompass everything that can in principle affect us, the observers of the universe. By "affect us" is meant become known to us by means of physical effects on either the observer, or the telescope, or on other bodies. This, then, is a definition of the physical universe. It excludes anything that is in principle undetectable physically, such as any metaphysical world, or heaven in the usual theological sense. It also excludes any regions of **spacetime** that are irreversibly cut off from our spacetime; these are properly called "other universes" and we can never know anything whatever about them.

The study of the universe at large is termed **cosmology**. Ideas about the properties of the universe are discussed under cosmological models.

Uranus

The seventh major planet from the Sun.

Uranus is usually visible only with the aid of a telescope. The maximum brightness it reaches is close to the limit of naked eye visibility. It was discovered by William Herschel in 1781. Telescopically, Uranus appears as a greenish-white disc. Even the best resolution reveals no surface features in photographs, though visual observers have reported faint belts. Uranus is markedly similar to the next major planet, Neptune. Uranus is 5 per cent larger, but 15 per cent less massive than Neptune. The greenish colour of both planets is caused by the methane present in their atmospheres.

Comparatively little is known about these more distant members of the Solar System because of the difficulty of observing them. Uranus' rotation period is uncertain, but its rotation axis lies only 8 degrees from orbital plane. When Uranus occulted a star in 1977, it was found that Uranus has a ring system, which is invisible to normal observation. It was detected only because the rings cut out the light from the distant star. They are probably similar in nature to Saturn's rings.

Uranus has five natural satellites. They are too small for their sizes to be measured directly, but their dimensions have been inferred from their brightness.

SATELLITES OF URANUS

number	name	probable diameter (km)	distance from Uranus (km)	orbital period (days)
V	Miranda	300	130,000	1.41
I	Ariel	800	192,000	2.52
II	Umbriel	600	267,000	4.14
III	Titania	1,100	438,000	8.71
IV	Oberon	1,000	586,000	13.46

See also: Solar System for table of planetary data.

V

Van Allen belts

Two zones encircling the Earth within which electrically charged particles are trapped.

The lower Van Allen radiation belts extend from about 1,000 to 5,000 km above the equator, and the upper belt is located at about 20,000 km. Within these zones electrically charged particles are trapped by the Earth's magnetic field. The particles

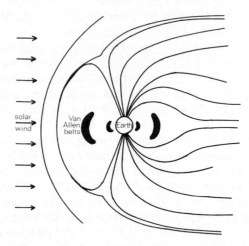

Fig. 27. The Earth's magnetosphere, showing the Van Allen belts where charged particles are trapped within the magnetic field.

themselves mainly come from the **solar wind**. The belts are named after James Van Allen, an American space scientist who discovered them in 1958.

See also: magnetosphere.

Variable star

A star whose luminosity is not constant, but varies with time, either regularly or irregularly.

Stars may vary in apparent magnitude for a number of reasons. The most fundamental distinction is between intrinsic and extrinsic variables. Intrinsic variables actually change their radiant output because of changes in the structures of the stars themselves. If a **binary system** happens to be positioned so that an observer on Earth sees one of the stars periodically pass in front and then behind the other, there will be a regular fluctuation in the observed brightness of the system. In this case, however, the variation is due to the chance orientation of the observer, and so has an extrinsic origin. A binary system of this type is said to be eclipsing.

All variable stars, other than the very brightest which have Greek letter names and possibly proper names as well, are given distinctive names based on the constellation in which they lie, and these names identify them immediately as variables. The brightest stars in each constellation are labelled α, β, γ, etc, usually in approximate order of diminishing brightness, followed by the genitive case of the Latin constellation name. For example, β Persei is the second most prominent star in the constellation Perseus. It also has the proper name Algol, and happens to be an eclipsing variable. Because of the chaotic way in which star naming was gradually extended to include letters of the Roman alphabet, the names of the less significant variables commence with R, S, T, etc. through to Z, then RR, RS, etc. to RZ, SS, ST, etc. to SZ and so on to ZZ. Further names are generated from the combinations AA to AZ, BB to BZ and so on to QZ, omitting J. Although this scheme provides names for 334 variables in each constellation, this is still not enough, so the more rational system of calling any further variables in a constellation V335, V336, etc. is used. Some examples of the names of variable stars are T Tauri, RR Lyrae, AY Hercules, and V339 Cygni.

Algol is the best known example of an eclipsing variable. The brightness of an eclipsing system usually shows two dips during the orbital period, corresponding to the primary star being in front and behind the secondary. The way the light output changes with time is called the light curve. Its precise shape contains information on the relative sizes and brightness of the two stars. Eclipsing binaries are important because they are the only double star systems where the angle at which they are being viewed can be inferred.

Intrinsic variables can be classified into various groups according to the mechanisms which cause their variations. Each group is known by its prototype, which is generally the brightest or the most intensively studied member of the group. Often, within a main group, subgroups may be identified. The properties of the main types of variables will be summarised in the following paragraphs.

T Tauri stars are yellow or orange **giants** which are believed to be very young stars, still condensing out of the interstellar material. They are found in associations which are evidently regions of star formation. Their **spectra**, which include emission lines, and a high level of infrared radiation can be understood in terms of the clouds of gas and dust which still surround these protostars. The variation is presumed to arise from movement of material and energetic activity, similar to solar **flares**, but on a larger scale.

Cepheid variables (prototype δ Cephei) are the main class of pulsating variables. The outer layers actually pulse in and out in a regular way. This movement shows up in the **Doppler** shift of spectrum lines. At the same time there is a regular fluctuation in brightness. The pulsation occurs because of an instability in the fine balance that holds a star together. This instability sets in when a star reaches a particular stage in its evolution. Cepheids have been of particular importance in astronomy because they act as distance indicators. There is a close correlation between the luminosity of Cepheid variables and their periods of variation which range between about one and fifty days. The more luminous the star, the longer its period. This relationship means essentially that it is only necessary to measure the period of variation of a Cepheid in order to determine its distance.

RR Lyrae stars are another class of pulsating variables which are also used for distance measurement. Like Cepheids, they are giants, but as a class are less luminous than Cepheids. They represent old stars which have consumed all the hydrogen in their cores and are starting to generate energy from reactions which use helium. They all have nearly the same absolute magnitude (about +0.5) so their distances may be inferred directly from their apparent magnitude. Their periods are shorter than Cepheids', ranging between 0.3 and 1.0 days.

Another major group of variables is formed by the **red giants** and **supergiants**. Betelgeuse (α Orionis) is a well-known example of an irregular red variable which changes in brightness only by a small amount. There are also red variables which fluctuate over a much greater range in a more regular way. Their prototype is Mira in the constellation Cetus. This spectacular variable has a range of about 8 magnitudes in the visible part of the spectrum.

Eruptive variables are subject to sudden, unpredictable outbursts, after which they fade again. **Novae** and **supernovae** fall into this category. A nova is the ejection of a shell of material by a star. A supernova is a catastrophic explosion of a massive star.

R Coronae Borealis is the prototype of a small group of supergiant stars that are the reverse of eruptive variables: they suffer large, sudden and unpredictable drops of brightness, then gradually recover their original luminosity. The explanation is thought to be the formation of solid particles of carbon in the cool outer layers. This "soot" blots out the light, until the build up of energy beneath it is able to blow away the obscuring material.

Venera program

A series of probes sent by the Soviet Union to explore the planet **Venus** since 1961.

Twelve Venera probes have been launched between 1961 and 1978. The huge atmospheric pressure on Venus, and its thick layer of opaque cloud have been major difficulties in the exploration of this planet. Venera 7 was the first to reach the surface, in 1970. Venera 9 returned the first photograph from the surface in 1975.

Venus

The second planet in sequence from the Sun.

Venus is the planet which attains the greatest brilliancy in the sky, reaching about −4.4 **magnitude**. It is seen either in the evening or early morning sky since its orbit lies inside the Earth's and its **elongation** from the Sun can never exceed 47°. Venus also exhibits **phases** as a consequence of its orbit lying within the Earth's. At greatest brilliancy Venus appears crescent-shaped, its nearness compensating for the fact that such a thin slice of the illuminated side is visible. Venus approaches nearer to the Earth than any other planet.

The visible disc is a blanket of thick opaque cloud which conceals all surface features on the rocky planet below. Space probes which have penetrated the atmosphere, such as the Soviet Venera series and the American **Pioneer** Venus 2, have returned data on the conditions below the clouds and radar has been used to map surface features.

The atmosphere is chiefly carbon dioxide and the pressure at the surface is over ninety times atmospheric pressure at the Earth's surface. The temperature is around 470°C at the ground, higher than on any other planet. The temperature is raised by the so-called "greenhouse" effect. Sunlight which penetrates the clouds warms the surface and is radiated back as infrared radiation at longer wavelengths. The clouds are opaque to this radiation, which cannot escape, so energy is trapped within the atmosphere raising the temperature to the high level observed. The clouds are composed of concentrated droplets of sulphuric acid and sulphur grains. Photographs taken in ultraviolet light show dark bands across the atmosphere which result from flow patterns.

The surface seems to be a rocky desert. Radar soundings have suggested the presence of mountains, craters and extinct volcanoes. A rift valley some 6 km deep and 400 km long has been detected. Venus has no significant magnetic field, and no natural satellites.

Vernal equinox see equinox

Viking program

Two American space probes which resulted in soft-landings on Mars in 1976.

Vikings 1 and 2 each consisted of a vehicle which was put into orbit around Mars, together with a Lander, which detached itself and descended to the surface. The missions included photography and experiments, such as meteorological and seismic recording. Of considerable interest were the tests performed on the soil in the hope of determining whether or not micro-organisms are present, but the results were inconclusive.

See also: Mars.

X

X-ray astronomy

The detection and analysis of cosmic X-rays.

X-ray astronomy is a recent arrival in the scene. The Earth's atmosphere is a formidable barrier to X-radiation. Consequently it is impossible to detect any X-rays from space using an instrument on the Earth's surface. After brief rocket flights in the 1960s, X-ray astronomy blossomed in the 1970s when detectors were put onto permanently-orbiting satellites. This technical development greatly increased the numbers and types of known cosmic X-ray sources. The domain of X-ray astronomy is generally considered to be from about 10 nanometres down to about 0.002 nanometres. X-radiation can be detected, for example, by devices sensitive to the ionisation that it causes.

Some 500 X-ray sources have been found. The brightest ones are **binary stars** in our **Galaxy** which are subject to mass exchange. A few can be matched to the remnants of old **supernovae.** Many of the active **galaxies** and **quasars** are faint X-ray sources.

Of particular interest are puzzling objects found in 1975 and known as X-ray bursters. These emit a sharp burst of X-rays that dies away after a minute or so. Possibly the bursts are triggered by spasmodic mass exchange in binary systems.

Y

Year

The time taken by the Earth to complete one orbit around the Sun.

It is possible to define the year precisely according to a number of reference points, but in each case the value is close to 365¼ days. The year which relates to the recurrence of the seasons is called the tropical year. Since the year is not an integral number of days it is necessary, for civil purposes, to adjust the number of whole days counted in a calendar year, by having an extra or leap day in the leap years. If this were not done, the seasons would get out of step with the calendar. Leap years occur when the year is exactly divisible by 4, except for years ending in 00 unless they are also divisible by 400. The year 2000 will be a leap year, but 1900 was not. This system was instituted by Pope Gregory XIII in 1582 and is now used throughout most of the world. The discrepancy between this system and the true length of the tropical year amounts to only 3 days in 10,000 years.

Z

Zenith

The point in the sky directly over an observer's head, which is thus 90° from all points on the horizon. The opposite point on the **celestial sphere**, beneath the observer's feet, is called the nadir.

Zodiac

The belt of twelve constellations forming a complete circle round the sky, through which the apparent paths of the Sun, Moon and planets pass.

The word zodiac is derived from the Greek zo-on, a living thing, and literally means "circle of creatures". Of the twelve constellations forming the zodiac, only one, Libra (the scales), is not now represented by an animal or human figure. The zodiacal **constellations** used today have their origin in the names used by the Babylonian astronomers of 600 B.C. or earlier, and the Greek equivalents of the present Latin names were in use by 2,000 years ago. Each constellation is also represented by a traditional symbol.

The significance of the zodiac lies in the fact that the motion of the Sun, Moon and planets against the background of distant stars is apparently confined to this narrow band encircling the sky. In fact, because of changes in the constellation boundaries, the path of the Sun (the **ecliptic**) now passes through part of the constellation Ophiucus as well as the twelve traditional zodiac constellations. According to the standard astronomical definition, the zodiac constellations are not all the same size, some being much larger than others. Astrologers, however, define their zodiac signs somewhat differently. They divide the circle of the zodiac into twelve equal sections, each 30° wide, which roughly correspond to the positions of the real constellations. The Sun spends about a month travelling through each sign, taking a year to complete an entire trip round the zodiac. Astrologers call the sign occupied by the Sun at the time of a person's birth their Sun sign. Astrology is generally regarded as a superstition by astronomers, and astrological interpretations must not be confused with the factual astronomical data on which they are based.

THE TWELVE TRADITIONAL CONSTELLATIONS OF THE ZODIAC

Latin name	English name	Symbol
Aries	Ram	♈
Taurus	Bull	♉
Gemini	Twins	♊
Cancer	Crab	♋
Leo	Lion	♌
Virgo	Virgin	♍
Libra	Scales	♎
Scorpio	Scorpion	♏
Sagittarius	Archer	♐
Capricornus	Goat	♑
Aquarius	Water carrier	♒
Pisces	Fish	♓

Zodiacal light

Sunlight scattered by small particles of dust lying in the plane of the Solar System, between the planets, causing a faint glow along the **zodiac** in the west after sunset and the east before sunrise.

The zodiacal light is so faint that it is usually only seen in tropical latitudes where the zodiac rises steeply from the horizon, and under conditions where the sky is extremely dark and moonless. It is mainly concentrated in zones about 20° either side of the Sun, and in a patch diametrically opposite the Sun, where it is called the counterglow, or **Gegenschein**, though its presence can be detected right round the zodiac.

Zwicky galaxy see galaxy